Linguistic Diversity

Linguistic Diversity

DANIEL NETTLE

OXFORD
UNIVERSITY PRESS

Great Clarendon Street, Oxford ox2 6DP

Oxford University Press is a department of the University of Oxford.
It furthers the University's objective of excellence in research, scholarship,
and education by publishing worldwide in

Oxford New York

Athens Auckland Bangkok Bogotá Buenos Aires Calcutta
Cape Town Chennai Dar es Salaam Delhi Florence Hong Kong Istanbul
Karachi Kuala Lumpur Madrid Melbourne Mexico City Mumbai
Nairobi Paris São Paulo Singapore Taipei Tokyo Toronto Warsaw
with associated companies in Berlin Ibadan

Oxford is a registered trade mark of Oxford University Press
in the UK and in certain other countries

Published in the United States
by Oxford University Press Inc., New York

British Library Cataloguing in Publication Data
Data available

Library of Congress Cataloging in Publication Data
Linguistic diversity / Daniel Nettle.
Includes bibliographical references and index.
1. Language and languages.   I. Title.
P106.N43   1999   400—dc21   98-53373
ISBN 0-19-823858-4 (hbk.)
ISBN 0-19-823857-6 (pbk.)

10 9 8 7 6 5 4 3 2 1

Typeset in Minion
by Regent Typesetting, London
Printed in Great Britain
on acid-free paper by
Bookcraft (Bath) Ltd., Midsomer Norton

Acknowledgements

The research on which this book is based was carried out whilst I was in the department of Anthropology at University College London, where I was supported by a Medical Research Council grant. It was prepared for publication whilst I was a postdoctoral fellow at Merton College, Oxford, for which opportunity I would like to thank the college's Warden and Fellows. I would also like to thank the organizers of the Human Diversity Project at King's College Research Centre, Cambridge, where I was a Visiting Fellow in the spring of 1998.

I thank Academic Press for permission to reproduce Figure 4.1, an earlier version of which appeared in my article 'Explaining Global Patterns of Language Diversity', *Journal of Anthropological Archaeology*, 17 (1998).

The professional debts I have incurred in writing this book are large and numerous. Special thanks go to Leslie Aiello and Robin Dunbar, who got me started on this track in the first place, helped me find out where it was going, and have continued to support and assist me throughout. Richard Hudson and Jim Hurford were enthusiastic and perceptive examiners; I hope the much-changed results of the work they have seen still meet with their approval. The ideas in the book have been commented on by readers both of the manuscript and of several related articles, by colleagues, and by audiences at a number of talks. I thank them all for their contributions. Some are anonymous. Those I can name include Bob Aunger, Rob Boyd, Elisabeth Cashdan, Chris Ehret, Rob Foley, Kathy Homewood, Simon Kirby, Chris Knight, Marta Lahr, Ruth Mace, Fritz Newmeyer, Camilla Power, Sara Randall, Colin Renfrew, Suzanne Romaine, Alan Rogers, Simon Strickland, and Maggie Tallerman. Lyle Campbell kindly gave me access to some of his as yet unpublished material. Tom Dickins read the entire manuscript whilst performing a 6c move out over an overhang. John Davey, my editor at Oxford University Press, injected enthusiasm when it was most needed. Time and my own cognitive limitations have conspired to prevent me incorporating all these people's suggestions, which would no doubt have strengthened everything contained herein. Needless to say, they would not necessarily agree with any of my conclusions, and all errors are entirely my own.

If these debts are great, then the gratitude I owe my friends and family is limitless. A few people must be singled out. In London: Adam, Alan, Cathy, Daisy, Emmanuel, Helen, Hilda, Jo, Pippa, Sian, Tania, and other Dan. In Oxford: Selina, Senia, Boye, Chris, Robin, Mark, and Alex. In Prague, which was the best of all: Martin, Tori, Justin, Andy, and the rest. Everywhere: Deborah, my brothers, Donna, and lastly Merrilyn. She inadvertently rescued this book when it was lying like a pole-axed wildebeest on the middle of my life.

D.N.

Oxford
August 1998

Contents

List of Figures

List of Tables

1 Introduction

> The diversity of languages, as they have been developed and adapted, is a
> patent fact of life that cries out for theoretical attention.
>
> (Hymes 1971: p. viii)

1.1 Preamble

Humankind today speaks about 6,500 different, mutually unintelligible
languages. These languages belong to at least 250 identifiable large families,
though there are various proposals to group these into still larger units. Within
these families, there are languages that use a dozen contrastive sounds, and
languages that use 100. There are languages that place the subject of the sentence
before the verb and languages that put the verb first. There are a few that place the
object before either. Some languages mark the relationships between the constituents of the sentence, or between the sentence and the world, by extensive
inflection, whilst others use almost none, and rely on independent particles and
the order of words.

This book is an investigation of these types of diversity in human language. For
each of the different kinds of diversity, we can ask a number of interesting
questions. First, why is there diversity at all? Secondly, why is there as much
diversity as there is, and why is it distributed as it is and not in some other
geographical pattern? The answer to the first question lies in the nature of
human language and the way it is used, while the answer to the second lies in the
study of history and prehistory, for the geographical distribution of linguistic
diversity is a product of the expansions, movements, and organization of human
societies through time. This book sets out to tackle both the first and the second
questions.

Interest in linguistic diversity as a topic has been growing over the last few
years. For the subfields of linguistic typology (Comrie 1989; Croft 1990), linguistic prehistory (Nichols 1990, 1992, 1997; Renfrew 1991; Bellwood 1997), and
language endangerment (Robins and Uhlenbeck 1991; Grenoble and Whaley
1998), diversity is the crucial variable to be explained. However, each of these
literatures concerns just one aspect of linguistic diversity—the grammatical, the
temporal, or the social—and these various factors have never been brought
together in a single framework. Nor is the phenomenon of diversity always

pursued right back to its ultimate causes, with many investigations instead content to note correlations between two linguistic parameters or between a linguistic one and a social one. A broad theory of diversity is thus still needed.

To an earlier generation of linguists, diversity seemed so natural as to require no explanation. For Edward Sapir, for example, language was

> a human activity that varies without assignable limit . . . from social group to social group, because it is a purely historical heritage of the group, the product of long-continued social usage. It varies as all creative effort varies—not as consciously, perhaps, but none the less as truly as do the religions, the beliefs, the customs, and the arts of different peoples. Walking is an organic, an instinctive function . . . speech is a non-instinctive, acquired, 'cultural' function.   (Sapir 1921/1970: 4)

Purely cultural inventions, such as legal systems and currencies, are of course different across different societies, as they have been developed separately at different times and under different conditions. Thus diversity requires no special explanation. However, most linguists today no longer believe that language is a cultural invention. On the contrary, it is held that the production, perception, and acquisition of language are controlled by highly specialized circuits in our brains that are common to all normal members of the species, and are probably specified in our genes to some extent. For modern linguistics, then, 'language is no more of a cultural invention than is upright posture. . . . Instead, it is a distinct piece of the biological makeup of our brains' (Pinker 1994: 18).

Now if the language faculty is a general biological attribute of our species, the fact of local diversity is extremely puzzling, for two reasons. First, the brain mechanisms of language learning and structure are presumably identical in all human populations. It is in virtue of this that any child growing up in any culture can acquire the relevant language so quickly and effortlessly. This makes it rather anomalous that there should be such differences between the final language systems of the English, the Edo, and the Enga that they cannot understand each other. We might expect differences in vocabulary reflecting differences in life style and material culture, just as blacksmiths and carpenters have different sets of terms specific to their activities. What we would not particularly expect, but do in fact find, are phonetic, phonological, and grammatical differences that seem entirely unmotivated by differences in situation or life style.

The second reason why it is puzzling to find linguistic diversity between human populations is that the depth of separation between them is not very great. Genetic evidence suggests that the entire species is descended from an ancestral population that was very small until comparatively recently (Stoneking 1993; Rogers and Jorde 1995). It seems that a common human ancestor lived as little as 140,000 years ago (see Relethford 1995: 59; though the implications of this finding for the origin of our species are not simple, since genetic coalescence dates have no necessary relationship with speciation events). Assuming a generation time of twenty-five years, that is only 5,600 generations ago. In view of the small population size (and perhaps geographic localization) that must have characterized humanity at this time, it seems likely that all the 6,500 contemporary languages, with all the diversity that they contain, as well as all those that have died out before now, have evolved in no more than this time period.

For such diversity to appear in such a short time suggests that powerful diversifying mechanisms are at work. Evidently those mechanisms have not been equally important in all times and all places. If Great Britain had the same ratio of spoken languages to inhabitants as Cameroon, it would have 1,250 native languages; if the United States had the same ratio as Papua New Guinea, it would have nearly 60,000. On the other hand, the total number of languages in the world is now in catastrophic and accelerating decline. We need, then, to understand both the forces that produce linguistic diversity and those that destroy it.

The contemporary emphasis in synchronic linguistics on the universal nature of language, then, actually makes diversity an important and surprising fact that requires further investigation. In the next sections I consider the theoretical tools that we have to undertake the task, and then the types of diversity that we encounter in the world.

1.2. The Family-Tree Model

The great result of nineteenth-century linguistics was the demonstration that many languages of Europe and Asia had a common origin in an extinct ancestral language from which they had ramified like the branches of a tree. The processes by which this had occurred were so regular that the shape of the tree could still be discerned and, even more intriguingly, the characteristics of the ancestral language tentatively reconstructed.

Thus the modern notion of the language family came about. A language family, or a stock, as we shall call it later, is a group of related languages that can be placed in a tree, and must be descended from a common ancestor of which we usually have no record, but about whose characteristics we can make some inferences. The first established and still best-studied example of such a family is Indo-European, which includes under its broad canopy most of the languages of Europe, Iran, and northern India.

Fuelled by their success with the Indo-European and Semitic languages, the family concept and the family-tree model became the organizing paradigm of historical linguistics. In much subsequent literature, then, to explain the diversity of an area has simply meant to reduce a large number of languages to a smaller number of families, and perhaps offer a sketchy tree for the families proposed. Larger families and families of families have been sought out. The early successes of the approach have not been sustained, though: for most parts of the world the number of families recognized is large (and controversial), the internal geometry of their trees very unclear, and their proto-languages unreconstructed.

In this book, the explanation of linguistic diversity will not mean the search for deep families and family trees. Indeed, there will be little discussion of the classical topics of historical linguistics, such as the regularity of sound change, reconstruction of proto-languages, and so on (for these matters, the reader is referred to any competent textbook such as Trask 1996 or Campbell 1998). This neglect is for two reasons.

First, historical linguistics, or at least that part of it concerned with family trees and reconstruction, is really about *how* languages diverge. It has relatively little to say about *why* they diverge (Campbell 1998: 282), which is our interest here. Even when neat trees are drawn and families established, many of the questions that are of interest in this book are left unanswered. Why did a particular family split into the number of descendants it produced? It was a unified language at one time; why did it not remain so, but split into three or eight of thirty-one separate communities? If languages are always ramifying, then the number of languages in the world should always increase, unless languages also go extinct. In fact, the number is not increasing, and languages are dying out, but we need to know which ones and why. We would also like to know what governs the rate at which languages diverge, and why they diverge in the fairly regular, structural ways that they do and not in some other, entirely different, way. Such questions must take us beyond the ken of historical linguistics and into the realms of other disciplines, as we shall see in Section 1.6; as Lehmann (1962: 200) put it, 'a linguist establishes the facts of change, leaving its explanation to the anthropologist'.

The second reason that the central notion of this book is not the family tree is that, although useful for understanding some types of diversity, the tree model of languages can be misleading for others. This is because languages change by processes of diffusion as well as treelike descent.

Central to the family-tree model is a metaphor of language as a living organism, and an asexual one at that. Thus the starting language produces daughter languages that are not quite the same as it; the daughters produce granddaughters that share their mother's idiosyncrasies but each add a few more of their own. This is very similar to Darwin's account of the evolution of animal species by descent with modification, and indeed the similarity is not accidental, since the discovery of the correspondences amongst the Indo-European languages was in Darwin's intellectual background. He comments in *The Descent of Man*: 'The formation of different languages and of distinct species, and the proof that both have been developed through a gradual process, are curiously parallel. . . . Languages, like species, can be classed in groups under groups, either naturally according to descent, or artificially by other characters . . .' (Darwin 1871: 465).

The assumption in Darwin's words and in the family-tree idea more generally is that each language is an integral entity that evolves by descent with a little internally generated modification. From time to time there are splits between languages caused, for example, by the speakers becoming separated by natural barriers, and thereafter there is no contact between them, and any modifications arising in the one are not transmitted to the other.

The main problem with the family-tree model, though it provides a good description at a macroscopic level of what happened to certain language families such as Indo-European, is that is does not accommodate all types of linguistic change. Languages are not phylogenetically homogeneous units; instead, their traits often derive from multiple sources in a way that depends on the origin and cultural affiliations of their speakers. I shall give examples below. In order to capture this fact, I will, therefore, present an alternative conceptualization of linguistic diversity, also using a biological analogy, that will be more useful in our investigations. This conceptualization is based on the notions of the linguistic item and the linguistic pool.

1.3. The Linguistic Item and the Linguistic Pool

I would like to introduce the notion that there is a human linguistic pool. This is an abstract entity analogous to the human gene pool. It contains all the different bits of linguistic structure that are found in human languages. The atomic elements in the pool, then, are not languages but linguistic items (in the sense of Hudson 1996: 21). A linguistic item is any piece of structure that can be independently learned and therefore transmitted from one speaker to another, or from one language to another. Words are the most obvious linguistic items, but sounds and phonological processes are items too, as are grammatical patterns and constructions. Vowel harmony, for example, must be an item, since there are dialects of Greek in Asia Minor that have gained vowel harmony from Turkish without also gaining the entire stock of Turkish words (Campbell 1998: 74).

No great claim need be made about the cognitive representation of items; the nature of the units that are represented in the mind/brain of language users is a matter of ongoing controversy, and is unlikely to be quickly resolved. Likewise, one can do population genetics or epidemiology without detailed knowledge of the biochemical realization of the traits or diseases whose distribution is under study. What matters for our purposes, as for the population geneticist or epidemiologist, is that linguistic items are potential *replicators*; that is, they could independently pass from one speaker, via the arena of language use, to another. The distributions of different items in the world's languages need not be statistically independent, and indeed very often are not. Groups of words, or of grammatical patterns, are found together, and such covariation is what linguistic typology and historical linguistics seek to explain, by reference either to history or to functional linkage between items, as we shall see.

The item as described here may seem a slightly unfamiliar unit, but in fact such a concept is tacitly present in all studies of languages in space and time, from dialectology and sociolinguistics to linguistic typology and areal linguistics. None of these endeavours could proceed if it did not identify the minimal traits over which speech forms can differ or converge from one point in space or time to the next.

In the linguistic pool there is evolution by descent with modification, but the evolving entities are not languages but individual items. Some items are rare and some are common, and we can place them in phylogenies, though in some cases there may be examples of the same item evolving several times independently. What have we gained by this shift of perspective from the language to the item? The answer is that we can account more generally for similarities and differences between human speech communities. What have we lost? Well, the item approach has one drawback that I feel can be easily overcome and that I discuss below.

Let us take a simple example of why the item approach is more inclusive than the language approach. Phylogenies can be drawn relating most English words to similar items in other European languages. Most of these phylogenies would show the English form branching most recently from the German and Dutch forms, as in the case of English *cow*, which is closer to German *kuh* than any French form. Thus most of the phylogenies for individual items would support the comparative linguist's normal view that English as a whole branched from a Germanic ancestor much more recently than its last common ancestor with French. However, a residue of forms would show the opposite patterning; English *beef* is clearly closely related to French *bœuf* and not to any Germanic form. Further investigation would reveal that most of the culinary terms in English have indeed come from French in waves of borrowing that reflect first the Norman Conquest and secondly the cultural importance of the French in this and other aristocratic domains.

This is where the analogy between an asexually evolving animal lineage and languages stops. Viewing languages as the evolving units does not allow mixing to be accounted for. Since most basic items in English are Germanic, English is assigned to the Germanic branch, and the residue of French items must be dismissed as so much noise in the data. From an item-based perspective, borrowing presents no problem. We can say that the English population is closely affiliated to the German one, but that there has also been a flow of items from the adjacent French population associated with certain demographic and cultural interactions.

Diffusion is not limited to individual words, but may also occur with grammatical patterns. In the Nigerian language Fyem, for example, there are five classes of noun, each of which forms its plural in a different way. Fyem is a Niger-Congo language by the common criterion of relatedness, and three of the plural formation types are also found in other Niger-Congo languages. A fourth type, however, is characteristic of a local family of Afroasiatic languages, whose speakers the Fyem often marry. The fifth type is widespread in both Niger-Congo and Afroasiatic languages of the region (see Nettle 1998*a*: ch. 8, for details of the Fyem case). In this case we have to say that the fourth pluralization type in Fyem is phylogenetically related, *as an item*, to the corresponding Afroasiatic item, since it came into the Fyem world through speakers from those languages. However, the Fyem language as a whole is not phylogenetically related to Afroasiatic, since most of the set of the items that make it up are not so descended. Thus our classification of Fyem as Niger-Congo is really a simplification that hides the true, mixed nature of its parentage.

The fact that individual grammatical items can pass between languages that are unrelated in the conventional sense means that there are many linguistic patterns in the world that are not explicable in the conventional family-tree framework. These are known in the literature as linguistic areas; well-known examples are the Balkans, where several key grammatical and phonological patterns cut across several branches of Indo-European and unrelated Turkish; south Asia, with diffused traits linking Indo-European, Munda, Tibeto-Burman and Dravidian, and Mesoamerica, with ten different families and isolates linked by diffused traits (Campbell *et al.* 1986).

At a larger scale, certain items are common in some continents and rare in others in a way that cuts across all identifiable family boundaries (Nichols 1992). Tonality is almost universal in Africa and south-east Asia, but rarer in all other continents. Clause alignment in most languages of the world is based on the nominative/accusative distinction (see Nichols 1992: 65–9 for an explanation). The polar opposite, ergativity, is rather common in the Pacific and Australia but rare elsewhere, whereas languages distinguishing two types of transitive verbs, one of which aligns ergatively and one accusatively, are very common in the Americas. Whether these large patterns represent ancient echoes of the founding populations of the continents, or the effects of long-term areal convergence, we cannot at present say.

Historical linguistics has, of course, always acknowledged the importance of diffusion and borrowing, which can extend not just to individual words but to any type of item. The existence of linguistic areas has long been recognized. However, the fact remains that the only widely used theoretical *model* that exists in historical linguistics is that of the family tree (though see Dixon 1997 for some suggestions towards alternatives). Borrowing and areal phenomena are just noted *post hoc*, and treated as reasons why trees, the basic construct, might be difficult to establish. The assumption remains that the most important component of variation in a set of speech norms will be treelike and reflect descent. It is not obvious a priori that this assumption is justified.

The existence of shared linguistic items between two populations is, then, evidence of some connection (though there is a possibility of independent evolution if the number of shared items is small), but the nature of this connection varies. Some items are diagnostic of the descent of two languages from a single common ancestor; if whole morphological paradigms are shared, for example, this is the most likely explanation. Other items suggest other kinds of cultural or demographic contact; the word order of languages, for example, tends to converge readily when individuals are bilingual in them. The item approach allows us to capture all types of linguistic change in a single framework.

We can ask, though, how the more familiar constructs of the language and the language family can be retained within an item-based approach. First, within the linguistic pool, there are sets of items which tend to co-occur. That is, speakers who have one of the set have a very high probability of having all the others. These sets are, of course, rather fuzzy, which is to say that some items in the set are only intermittently present or variable in their form, and the composition of the set changes over time. At a given moment, though, where there is a set that is sufficiently different from all other sets that its speakers cannot be understood by anyone else, we say that we have a separate language. I will return to the problems with such a definition of the language in Chapter 4. For now, I will simply accept it.

Now children are often acculturated by a community who mostly have the same set of linguistic items. Thus the set will be passed on as a set, though small modifications will become incorporated for reasons we will discuss in Chapter 2. Where sub-communities become separated, their sets of items will thus diverge, giving the conventional family tree of languages. The language family is thus any group of sets of items that can be placed in a phylogeny. Note that in the item-based framework there is no guarantee that a family tree or a single-parent family will exist for a given language. To the extent that children are acculturated by adults with a mixture of different item sets, languages can be mixed.

In fact, historical linguists have managed to produce family trees of some sort for almost all of the world's languages. This does not mean that item flow between languages, or admixture, is rare. Admixture is omnipresent. However, in most cases, a main line can be identified, which represents the evolutionary pathway of *most* of the items in a language.[1] This is the phylogeny routinely put forward as being that of the whole language. The utility of such a procedure depends on the extent of the admixture. Where admixture accounts for a small proportion of total change, the family tree is informative. Where the admixture has been overwhelmingly important, then trying to draw a single phylogeny for the whole language may become a pointless exercise. This is clearly the case with Creoles and radically mixed languages such as Anglo-Romani and Michif (Thomason and Kaufman 1988; see also Bakker and Mous 1994), but it may not be restricted to extreme situations. For the case of Fyem, for example, I argued that more could

---

[1] In fact, in the establishment of phylogenetic relatedness, not all items weigh equally, since there is a core of items that are clearly more phylogenetically conservative than others.

be discovered of the Fyem past by studying patterns of admixture than by trying to bludgeon the data into a family tree (Nettle 1998*a*), and similar problems with trees have been reported by scholars studying many different regions (e.g. for Africa, Dimmendaal 1995; for Australia, Dixon 1997; for the Pacific, Grace 1996, Ross 1996).

What historical linguistics has generally failed to consider, until very recently, is that the extent to which the variation in a set of languages is treelike is itself a datum of interest, and ways of measuring this should be devised. A treelike structure bears witness to a rapid geographical or demographic expansion of one group, perhaps associated with economic changes in prehistory; a less dendritic structure suggests various possibilities, such as a long period of *in situ* evolution with high rates of exogamy, or extensive multilingualism (Dixon 1997). Thus the fact that such a good family tree can be produced for Indo-European and Bantu is not just a piece of good fortune but a piece of information about prehistory, and the fact that no such tree can be established in Australia is not a nuisance but a finding.

At the beginning of this section I mentioned that the linguistic-item approach to diversity had drawbacks as well as advantages. The principal drawback is the following: in the history of languages, items do not change independently, as we shall see in later chapters. Instead, they are to some extent coordinated in a system. This was the basic positive insight of structuralism. A classic example is that of vowel systems (Martinet 1955; Disner 1984). However many vowel sounds a language has, they will tend to be organized in such a way as to be as distant as possible from each other within phonetic and acoustic space. If one vowel sound undergoes historical change, then it will often cause the others to move in a co-ordinated way, so that in the end optimal spacing will be re-established. The chains of vowel movement so caused can be extremely complex and last several hundred years, as has happened in modern English (see Labov 1994 for a full discussion).

This coordination amongst items is to be expected if languages are seen as organic wholes. However, I believe it can be captured equally well from an item-based perspective. Items are separable, but their evolutionary trajectories are affected by other items around them. In the same way, the evolutionary trajectory of a given animal will depend heavily on which other animals and plants are around. Thus there are emergent regularities in nature at the level of the ecosystem or the ecological community. Languages are just the same; every item evolves in an ecosystem formed by the other items around it in the linguistic pool. There are emergent regularities at the language level, which the behaviour of vowel systems illustrate, because of this ecological linkage. It seems, though, that the item approach can capture both the mixability of languages and their internal coherence.

1.4. Levels of Diversity in the Linguistic Pool

We have now introduced the notions of the linguistic item and the linguistic pool that will serve as our conceptual framework for the whole book, and shown how the familiar concepts of the language and language family can be derived from them. In this section I will argue that three different types of diversity can be identified in the human linguistic pool. Each of these types shows a different pattern and requires a different explanation. The remainder of the book will be devoted to those patterns and explanations.

The first type of diversity is simply the number of different languages in a given geographical area. Papua New Guinea and Paraguay are roughly the same size and have nearly the same population, but Papua New Guinea has over 850 indigenous languages, whilst Paraguay has scarcely more than twenty. Papua New Guinea is clearly more diverse in this sense. I call this type of diversity *language diversity*.

The second type of diversity we wish to identify is *phylogenetic diversity*. This is the number of different lineages of languages found in an area. It can be measured at various levels—that of the subfamily of languages, or that of a higher phylogenetic node such as the stock (Nichols 1990: 477–9). There is no necessary correlation between language diversity and phylogenetic diversity. Central Africa is extremely high in language diversity, but almost all of the languages belong to the Bantu family of Niger-Congo. Thus the region is rather poor in diversity at all phylogenetic levels higher than the language itself. Tropical South America, on the other hand, is not particularly high in language diversity but contains representatives of dozens of language families. It is, therefore, high in phylogenetic diversity.

The third and final type of diversity is *structural diversity*. It seems that there are certain fundamental loci in the structure of every language that must be filled, and there are a number of alleles (alternative items) for these loci that are found in the language pool. For example, in the ordering of the major constituents (Verb, Subject, Object), languages can favour the verb first (e.g. VSO, as is found in Maasai), verb second (e.g. SVO, as in English), verb finality (e.g. SOV, as in Khalkha Mongolian), or free order. Now the structural diversity of a particular region on some parameter is the extent to which its languages vary on that parameter. This is potentially independent of both the language diversity and the phylogenetic diversity of the region, since there are parameters, such as word order, on which languages of the same family differ, and languages of completely different families often converge. Structural diversity is thus an independent dimension of diversity in the language pool.

The distinction between the three levels of linguistic diversity forms the backbone of this book. For each type of diversity, we ask how much diversity there is, how it is distributed, and why it has evolved. Chapters 4 and 5 are devoted to language diversity, Chapter 6 to phylogenetic diversity, and Chapter 7 to structural diversity. Before embarking on those investigations, some preliminaries are in order. In the remainder of this chapter I briefly discuss my general approach, and in the next chapter I set the scene for the subsequent ones by asking why there is any diversity in language at all—in other words, what the mechanisms are which cause human languages to diversify.

1.5. Justification, Disguised as Apology

As the reader may have remarked, the questions to be tackled in this book are of a very general nature, and I approach them at a macroscopic level. Attempting to survey such a broad remit in a single swoop may appear to exceed the bounds of good sense. After all, the causes and pathways of language diversification in Mexico may be quite different from those that obtain in Melanesia, and any attempt to subsume them under some kind of universal schema might obscure more than it reveals. In my defence, I would argue that asking very general questions is not only interesting, but is a valid strategy in the pursuit of knowledge.

Science does not proceed by a steady accumulation of facts. It is rather an intermittent sequence, consisting alternately of the setting-out of broad frameworks for understanding phenomena, and the execution of extremely detailed empirical studies that may show those frameworks to be inadequate. There is surprisingly little contemporary literature on the reasons for linguistic diversity, and so this book is intended to set out some broad theory. We cannot explain everything about the distribution of the three types of diversity, or even come close. I hope instead to clarify the *main* factors involved, and the *kinds* of answers we would expect where as yet we have none. More detailed studies of individual languages and individual communities will be needed to put some flesh on the bones discussed here. Without having some bones first, however, you can do nothing with flesh except leave it in a heap. I therefore apologize to anthropologists for the broad generalizations about societies made in Chapters 4 and 5, to theoretical linguists for the simplistic view of linguistic change in Chapters 3 and 7, and so on. One cannot simultaneously maximize precision and generality. The former is rather traded off against the latter. I have tried to retain sufficient precision for the results to be meaningful, by subjecting all the hypotheses put forward to rigorous quantitative tests, but this book is unavoidably at the high-generality end of the continuum.

Methodologically, too, the approach used here may seem unfamiliar, particularly to linguists and linguistic anthropologists. Studies in those disciplines often proceed inductively, characterizing the situation in a particular language or society, and then perhaps moving on to see if the same holds true in some other area. Sampling is opportunistic, data are introduced anecdotally, methods are qualitative, and no clear division is made between the generation of hypotheses and their testing. Now this kind of inductive methodology can surely provide useful insight and generalizations about language and society. However, it is perhaps overly concerned with the single case, and has difficulty furnishing general explanatory hypotheses, let alone testing them (and indeed, for these reasons, sub-fields of linguistics such as typology have had to abandon them for more formal methods).

The methodology used in this book is somewhat different, and will be more familiar to evolutionary biologists. Each chapter seeks a general model (ideally quantitative) of how some aspect of diversity may evolve. The predictions of that model are then tested statistically against quantitative data drawn from the literature on that topic. Both general models and large statistical data sets tend to alarm, perhaps justifiably, those working in the humanities tradition, with their nuanced qualitative knowledge of the single case. However, as I have made clear, there should be no conflict between these approaches. They should stimulate each other; they are the two sides of a dialectic.

1.6. The Need for an Interdisciplinary Approach

Linguistic diversity is, as I have said, an under-theorized topic. It falls through the gap between disciplines. Anthropologists and geographers tend to be mainly interested in language as a marker of social affiliation or historical origin, and so they are not much concerned with phoneme mergers or morphological reorganization, which are undeniably the province of linguistics. Historical linguistics deals with those processes, but makes no attempt to explain the social and geographical origins of diversity. Even in Nichols's (1992) path-breaking study, whose insights we shall be drawing on several times, the ultimate causes of diversity are relegated to 'external factors' that 'cannot figure in a linguistic model, except as unknowns' (Nichols 1992: 209). The way in which the languages of the world have diverged thus never receives a unitary treatment. It follows that any attempt at one, including the present thesis, *must* be interdisciplinary in its scope.

This book is primarily a work of linguistic anthropology rather than linguistics. Its aim is to elucidate how languages have diversified through space and time, and not to provide a framework for understanding the internal structure of language. Indeed, the present work presupposes that such frameworks are available, though they are not discussed in much detail. From time to time, though, I shall venture into the arena of language structure. This is mildly audacious; the separation between the sciences of society and the science of the structure of language has come to be very great, and linguists generally seem to assume that studying social, spatial, or historical patterns of language *use* is of little value for understanding language *structure*.

This attitude is part of a wider mentality in the human sciences that promotes compartmentalization. Reading professional journals or visiting universities, one would be forgiven for thinking that human beings engaged in a series of distinct, non-overlapping behaviours: economic behaviour, where they worked and gained money; social behaviour, where they associated with each other quite independently of their economic behaviour; linguistic behaviour, where they learned to produce utterances of various types quite independently of the social setting; cultural behaviour, where they performed strange acts determined by the invisible monolith of their culture, and so on. Of course, this is not true. Every economy is also a social and cultural system, and a language lives only because there is a society to speak it and a cultural framework that transmits it. Where an economy changes or a society changes composition, languages and cultures live, mutate, or die out, as we shall see.

In defence of compartmentalization, scholars argue that a premature attempt at reduction of phenomena in one domain to those in another leads to little understanding of either domain. Language, culture, and social systems all have an inherent logic of form and change that can be understood only by careful, perhaps comparative, study on their own terms. The great successes of the special human sciences, such as structuralism in linguistics, relied on a restriction of the domain of enquiry to a limited system, which turned out to have important internal regularities.

We must beware of a facile equivocation between description and explanation here. It may be true that linguistic structure must be *described* in its own terms, and cannot be ontologically reduced to system-external factors such as economics or general psychology. It does not follow that linguistic structure is to be *explained* without reference to external factors. Languages may be autonomous objects, but they are best viewed as objects of the third kind (Keller 1994). That is, they are obviously not natural objects (objects of the first kind). Nor are they deliberate human productions (objects of the second kind), since people do not intentionally create their languages. They are not even aware of most of the rules they effortlessly use or the linguistic changes in which they participate. However, this does not mean that the history of a language has nothing to do with the behaviour of speakers. Languages are still the consequences of speakers' actions, just not the outcome of their intentions. The structure of language has emerged from the kind of messages speakers wish to convey and the kind of cognitive, perceptual, and articulatory mechanisms they have to convey them, either by biological evolution, or by cultural evolution, or more likely by some combination of the two. Precisely the same is true of social and cultural systems; they must ultimately be seen as emergent consequences of individual people's adaptive behaviour in different circumstances (Herrmann-Pillath 1994).

Thus disciplinary boundaries, and those who are too quick to defend them, should be treated with suspicion. Even if it is true that, as Saussure contended, the object of linguistics is language studied 'in and for itself', it does not follow that the explanation should only be in terms of language. Nor should the explanation of social phenomena be limited to cultural rules. Faced with a phenomenon, our first step must always be to describe it on its own terms. We then explain it by showing how it emerged from forces which are more basic and better understood. I will thus be linking the distribution and evolution of languages to facts about social organization, and facts about social organization to the economic necessity of procuring subsistence in different environments. I thus concur with Thomason and Kaufman (1988: 4) that the history of a language should be treated as a function of the history of its speakers.

This strategy does not deny the valid distinction between the structure and the use of language. I merely believe that use can influence the evolution of structure, just as the ever-present pressures of climate and economy influence sociocultural systems. Compartmentalization has been useful for such disciplines as anthropology and linguistics, both methodologically, as it has allowed exact and rigorous characterizations of the phenomena at hand, and sociologically, as it has allowed them to emerge as distinctive intellectual communities. Ultimately, however, too much compartmentalization leaves the two disciplines like the Danae sisters of classical Greek mythology, each of whom was condemned forever to pour water into her own separate and bottomless container.[2] Linguistic diversity is at once a structural, a social, and an economic phenomenon, and so, to paraphrase William Labov, only a set of propositions that relate general findings about linguistic diversity to general properties of human beings or of human societies will deserve to be called a theory of linguistic diversity (after Labov 1994: 5).

---

[2] Wolf (1982: 11) attached this beautiful metaphor, which I have also borrowed elsewhere, to the social sciences in general.

2 Language Evolution: Basic Mechanisms

2.1. Introduction

The millions of species of the biological world have all gradually diverged from some inconceivably distant common ancestor. The lion and the cheetah share a relatively recent parent in an undifferentiated African big cat, but they have by now become so distinct that they can no longer interbreed, and would not ordinarily be mistaken for each other. The horse and the donkey have gone less far down the same road; they can still mate, but the resulting mules are sterile and thus unviable.

As we have seen, the history of human languages is also one of descent with modification, though I have argued that the evolving units are really items, with the language a derivative concept resulting from non-independence amongst sets of items. Why there should be divergence at all amongst the linguistic items used by humanity is in fact a more complex question than it seems at first blush. The candidate causes of change were already identifiable by the time Saussure wrote his *Cours*; but exactly how they worked was unclear, and Saussure concluded his discussion dismissively: 'Time changes all things; there is no reason why language should escape this universal law' (Saussure 1916: 114). This set the tone for much subsequent historical work, which has concerned itself with cataloguing and reconstructing how change proceeds, rather than investigating its causes. Indeed, until recently there seems to have been a tendency to be 'suspicious of questions beginning with the word "why", regarding them as a relic of childhood which mature scientists should have learned to put behind them' (Sampson 1980: 166; cf. Campbell 1998: 282). Thus we are still some distance from a general, integrated understanding of the mechanisms which cause linguistic divergence.

In biological evolution, the divergence of species occurs because of two types of mechanism. First, there are *sources of variation* between individuals. The main one of these is mutation, which is the tendency for a small proportion of animals' genetic material to change, at random, from generation to generation. Variation acting alone cannot produce distinct species. It just makes populations internally heterogeneous. For this heterogeneity to lead to divergence of species, a second group of mechanisms is required. These are the *amplifiers of variation*, which take the small differences between individuals and, over time, fixate and enlarge them until they become stable major differences between populations. Anything which prevents the variation that arises in one part of the population being transmitted to other parts is an amplifier, so geographical isolation, natural selection, and perhaps sexual selection can all play this role.

For linguistic evolution to be possible, too, there must be both sources and amplifiers of variation. In this chapter we consider what they are. In Section 2.2 I outline the simplest possible account of language change, which I shall call the neutral model. I will then argue that there are conceptual difficulties with such a simple model, and in Section 2.3 I explain what they are. In Section 2.4 I introduce the other, more complex factors that must be incorporated to provide a more realistic model of language change.

2.2. The Neutral Model

In this section I will present a very simple, almost caricatured, account of how language change works. The purpose of doing this is to show where the difficulties lie, and in the subsequent sections I will discuss these difficulties and what their solutions might be. I call the basic model presented here the neutral model, in partial reference to the neutral-mutation model of biological evolution (Kimura 1983). In that theory, species diverge because of a small rate of random genetic mutation (which is the source of variation), and geographical isolation (which is the amplifier). Genetic mutations in the theory are assumed to have no functional advantage to the individual carrying them (hence the term neutral). This last assumption is not strictly true. Many mutations must affect the fitness of their bearers one way or another (though what proportion do is impossible to determine). None the less, the neutral-mutation model is a useful baseline theory against which the actual dynamics of evolution may be compared. It has some particularly useful applications, such as the theory of molecular clocks, which allows estimation of the time since separation of related species through an assumed constancy in the rate of mutation.

The neutral model of language evolution presented here is very similar to the biological neutral-mutation model. However, the transmission of genes and the transmission of linguistic norms are really quite different, and so there are huge problems for the neutral linguistic model, to which I return in Section 2.3.

The neutral model works in the following way. Language is transmitted down the generations by children learning it and becoming users, and the next generation of children learning from them in turn. Language transmission is not perfect. Every new generation of speakers picks up some minor random variants. There are many possible variants, each of which has only a small probability of occurring and a much smaller probability of becoming generally adopted. In two different populations, then, it is highly improbable that exactly the same variants will crop up. It follows that, as long as two populations are geographically isolated, the variants they accumulate will be different and they will drift further and further apart until they are mutually unintelligible or even unrecognizable as related.

General accounts of language change rarely make their assumptions explicit, but, when they do, the underlying mechanism they assume often seems very close to this neutral model. Pinker (1994: 241–61), for example, explicitly adopts the vocabulary of random mutation and separation amongst groups of speakers. The neutral model is most clearly implicit in the well-known tools of comparative linguistics, lexicostatistics, and glottochronology (Swadesh 1950; reviewed by Embleton 1986, 1992).

Lexicostatistics assumes that basic words in the lexicon of a language are gradually replaced or made unrecognizable, one by one and at random, by processes of innovation. The proportion of basic words that are recognizably cognate in two languages thus gives a measure of the closeness of their relationship. Two languages that share 75 of the words on the list devised by lexicostatisticians are thus more closely related (that is, have a closer common ancestor) than two languages that share 50 or 25 of the words. This technique is supposed to allow the construction of family trees, just as DNA phylogenies can show the pattern of relatedness in groups of species. The frequency of admixture in the lexicon undermines the theoretical basis of lexicostatistics (Hoijer 1956; Teeter 1963), but it is such a simple technique to use that it refuses to die out altogether, and indeed can be a useful way of establishing preliminary hypotheses about relatedness.

Glottochronology makes the further assumption that the rate of lexical replacement is approximately constant. Thus, the number of replacements in the basic word list can give a measure of the time elapsed since two languages split. Glottochronology is thus the linguistic counterpart of the theory of molecular clocks. However, unlike the genetic case, where there is some evidence for the assumption that molecular evolution proceeds at a constant rate (reviewed by Kimura 1983), there is no good evidence for a constant rate in lexical change. In fact, it is unlikely to be at all constant, given the prevalence of admixture and the effect of social influences on language (see Bergslund and Vogt 1962; Dixon 1997; Nettle, forthcoming *b*). The dates given by glottochronology thus cannot be taken seriously.

The neutral model, then, is the simplest possible conceptualization of language change. In the next section I shall deal with the problems inherent in it, which fall into four groups. First, there are queries about what exactly the source of variation is. Secondly, there are what I shall call the averaging and threshold problems. Thirdly, there are questions about the importance of geographical isolation. Fourthly, the fact that changes in languages tend to be correlated has to be dealt with.

2.3. Problems with the Neutral Model

2.3.1. The source of variation

The possibility of linguistic variation arises because of the *discontinuity* of language transmission (Meillet 1926).[1] That is, the grammar in the head of older speakers does not reproduce itself directly in the head of younger ones. Instead, an indirect two-stage process occurs. First, adult speakers map their linguistic *competence* into actual linguistic *performance*. Linguistic competence may be defined as the set of abstract mental representations that constitute any speaker's mental grammar of their language. Linguistic performance is the actual set of utterances that is produced in real-time communicative situations. Secondly, learners are exposed to a finite sample of linguistic performance, and must map this back, via some kind of learning procedure, into their own competence in the language.

Variation can thus arise at both stages in this process. I will treat each in turn, to see if either can serve as the source of variation linguistic evolution requires.

In performance, grammatical systems interact with various other systems, such as the articulatory mechanisms that produce speech, attention, memory, and other cognitive systems. All of these systems can be responsible for discrepancies between speech output and the canonical grammatical form. Phonetic tokens of a particular item, for example, are not identical every time they are produced, but are quite widely scattered around the canonical value in phonetic space. They vary considerably in the speech of a single speaker according to the immediate phonological context (Rosner and Pickering 1991), and the wider social or communicative context (Lindblom *et al.* 1992). They vary dramatically between individuals, even those of broadly similar dialects (Peterson and Barney 1952). This variation is presumably due to the motor demands of actually producing the fast, coordinated stream of gestures that is speech in real time in a way that is coordinated with breathing and other behaviour.

---

[1] Discontinuity is a product of the fact that a significant component of language is transmitted culturally rather than genetically. It is not absurd to ask why this is the case. According to the innatist school in modern linguistics, language is as much a part of our biology as the echo-location system of the bat is a part of its biology (Pinker 1994: 19). If this view is correct, then the fact that *any* part of language is learned stands in need of explanation. In their classic statement of the 'biological' approach to language, Pinker and Bloom (1990) address the question of why this should be the case. They provide three reasons why there should be a learned component. First, to represent a complete language genetically might consume excessive space in the genotype. Secondly, as the language faculty must be expected to change by genetic drift (the accumulation of random mutations), an individual with an innate language might fall out of kilter with his peers. It would thus be advantageous to have a code with developmental flexibility to 'home in' on that spoken in the community. Thirdly, as Hinton and Nowlan (1987) find, once most of a trait is determined genetically, selective pressure to represent the rest in the genotype declines, because learning can be relied on to fill it in. There is thus no fitness advantage to mutations that provide further innate knowledge of language.

Variation is not just phonetic. Lexical items are used in novel and idiosyncratic ways as speakers search to express the meanings they seek on-line under the constraints of memory, attention, and so forth. Many grammatical constructions in performance deviate from the canonical form of the language. When corpora of real everyday speech are analysed, utterances deviating from canonical forms on all major grammatical dimensions are found, at a low but significant frequency (Carter and McCarthy 1995). Thus, in linguistic performance, the variation is there for the language to change from its present structure in any direction, if the variants were only able to become fixed (and we will come to the problem of how variants do get fixed below).

Some linguistic variants will be one-offs, restricted to a single utterance, whilst others may recur reasonably often, either as typical of an individual or as typical of a particular linguistic context. It could be argued that such variation is only partially akin to genetic mutation. Genetic mutation is entirely random; that is, a mutant gene that is extremely useful is no more likely to arise than one that is lethal or one that has no effect at all. With variation in speech production, this is not obviously the case. Speech production is a goal-directed activity, and speakers are more likely to produce variants that facilitate production and easy communication than those that do not. Phonetic variants where nasalization spreads from a nasal consonant to an adjoining vowel, or voicing spreads from a vowel to an adjoining consonant, will thus be likely to occur, whereas variants where velar consonants cause nasalization of the following vowel will not. Similarly, if memory load exerts a pressure on the form of utterances, then it will be only towards simpler ones and never in the other direction, and thus it is a form of directed, not random, mutation.

If mutation is too predictable, the neutral model does not work as an explanation of diversity. The whole reason that diversity appears in that model is that there are large numbers of possible variants, each of which has an equal, but low, probability of cropping up. If the series of mutations that arose was deterministic, then ever-increasing diversity would not be assured, as the same series of innovations would show up independently in population after population. Languages would change, but all in the same direction.

I think that this problem may safely be put to one side. Performance factors do lead to directional types of change, as we shall see in Section 2.3.2, and the variation they produce is not truly random. However, it is almost certainly sufficiently pseudo-random for a neutral model to work. This is because there are many competing demands on speech production. The demands of the articulatory system tend to produce phonetic reduction of words, and massive coarticulation of segments, but one's pragmatic desire to be understood favours maximal elaboration and clarity of the speech signal. Natural articulatory tendencies may favour spreading nasalization from a consonant to an adjoining vowel, but the speaker may also override this tendency to get his meaning across in an ambiguous situation. The desire to be as informative and coherent as possible in discourse may well lead to long utterances that are hard to parse and have high memory demands, whereas simpler, shorter sentences may lack the desired informational richness and flow. In short, production is moulded by multiple pressures that pull in opposing directions, and that no doubt vary in strength from moment to moment. The result will, therefore, be a pattern of variation about the canonical form that is quite unpredictable and unrepeatable. When one adds that the subset of variants that actually get adopted into the grammar of any language is also subject to many factors and some pure chance, it seems that the process is sufficiently close to randomness for the neutral model to work.

The second stage in the process of language transmission where variation can arise is in acquisition. It has often been assumed that acquisition is not perfect: 'If languages were learnt perfectly by the children of each generation, then languages would not change. . . . The changes in languages are simply slight mistakes, which in the course of the generations completely alter the character of the language' (Henry Sweet, quoted in Aitchison 1991: 165).

The argument that learning is imperfect became an orthodoxy in the classical period of historical linguistics in the late nineteenth century (see Baron 1977: 19–21), and has enjoyed somewhat of a resurgence in recent theory (see e.g. King 1969; Andersen 1978). Imperfect learning is clearly a powerful potential source of variation, as, unlike performance variants that can be one-off, variants due to it will always be used by the speaker in question.

The question again arises of whether imperfect learning is really akin to random mutation. It is likely that certain structures are more likely to be mislearnt than others, and the pattern of mislearning will not be random. Nineteenth-century historical linguists invoked imperfect learning to account for the persistent trend towards morphological simplification in the Indo-European languages. In more recent theory, too, it has been assumed that imperfect learning will always entail simplification of rule systems. For example, a regular plural form (*iguanas*) is easier to acquire than an irregular one (*sheep*). Indeed, the regular form requires no particular acquisition at all; the structure of English will lead to it being inferred even in the absence of examples. Children in fact go through a stage of over-regularizing forms like *sheep* (to *sheeps*), and must learn to retreat from this overgeneralization. Now imperfect learning is much more likely to result in a failure to obtain the exception than a failure to acquire regular forms. It should thus have definite directional effects in the history of languages. The class of irregular plurals should gradually shrink at the expense of the class of regular ones.

If mislearning exerts such directional effects, then it is not an equivalent of random mutation at all, but much closer to an equivalent of natural selection. I shall discuss acquisitional biases again under the heading of functional selection, in Section 2.4.2. However, there are probably circumstances under which imperfect learning can operate in many directions, towards elaboration as well as towards simplification (Baron 1977). For example, children can acquire a rule but fail to acquire constraints on its operation. The classes of edible sea fish and anglable freshwater fish, for example, have zero plurals in English (*haddock, cod, perch, trout,* cf. *whales, stingrays, minnows, guppies*). A learner could easily fail to acquire the restriction and generalize the rule to all common fish names (this may explain such forms as *goldfish*).[2] In other words, though mislearning may consistently simplify the underlying rule system, it may lead to changes that do not simplify the surface structure of the language. Overall, the changes produced by imperfect learning are very likely to be non-deterministic or pseudo-random, which is all the neutral model requires.

Performance and acquisition, then, provide the sources of variation that are necessary for language to change. There are unanswered questions about how these mechanisms work in detail, but, since there is abundant variation and change in language, it is clear that they do work. There are also question marks over whether variation stemming from performance or acquisition factors is truly random. However, as we have seen, it is probably sufficiently unpredictable for the neutral model to work. We now turn to more serious problems with the model, which stem from the way language is inherited.

2.3.2. The averaging and threshold problems

We have seen in the previous section that there are sources of unpredictable variation in linguistic systems, as the neutral-mutation model requires. For distinct languages to evolve, the variants produced must get adopted into the linguistic system and passed on to new individuals. In biological evolution, once a new mutation arises, it will be more or less automatically passed on. An offspring's genes are inherited from the parents, all in a bundle in asexual species, and by a shuffling of half of the material from each parent in sexual species. Thus a new mutation is bound to be passed on to any given descendant in the asexual case, and has a 50 percent chance in the sexual case. (I am assuming, of course, that the bearer of the mutation survives to have a descendant. This would not be true if the mutation concerned was lethal; however, following Kimura's argument, I consider for the moment only mutations that have no effect on reproductive success.) In linguistic evolution, it is not so straightforward for new mutations to be passed on, because of differences between the way languages are inherited, which is by social learning, and the way genes are inherited. In fact, most mutations are unlikely ever to make it into the linguistic systems of new

---

[2] Other exceptions such as *eels* and *sharks* may stem from marginal edibility and/or marginal fishness.

speakers. The reasons why this is so can be termed the 'averaging' and 'threshold' problems.

Individuals do not learn language just from their parents, but from many people. An individual's peer group seems to be the most important influence. Children learn language partly in order to keep in kilter with the speech norms of their social group. It is, therefore, reasonable to assume that, during language acquisition, they will home in as accurately as possible on the speech going on around them. The optimum learning strategy for them would, therefore, be some kind of error-minimizing procedure—that is, an algorithm for minimizing the discrepancy between the child's own speech and that which it hears going on around it.

Error-minimizing strategies of this kind are likely to lead to children producing a statistical composite of the speech they experience, and such a process seems prone to erase all the random variation that has arisen. To see why this is the case, let us take a couple of specific examples.

Any vowel segment in any language has a typical phonetic value. For example, let us say that the English segment /e/ is typically realized as a harmonic sound with a first formant frequency of 500hz and a second format frequency of 1,550hz. Let us also say that any child acquiring English encounters lots of variation around this average value, both between individuals, and also between utterances by the same individual, for the reasons we have already discussed. If the degree and direction of all the variation are effectively random, then it may reasonably be expected that they will be mutually cancelling in the large set of data that constitutes the child's linguistic experience. The child will, therefore, acquire none other than the canonical value of 500hz/1,550hz.

This is the *averaging problem*: on average, random changes in continuous linguistic variables sum to zero, leading to no change. This problem was clearly understood as long ago as Sapir's *Language*:

The explanation of primary dialectic differences is still to seek . . . If all the individual variations within a dialect are being constantly levelled out to the dialect norm . . . why should we have dialect differences at all? Ought not the individual variations of each locality, even in the absence of intercourse between them, to cancel out to the same accepted speech average?   (Sapir 1921/1970: 149–50)

Most linguistic variables are not continuous but discrete. That is, unlike the gradation of vowel quality, they involve a straight choice between a pair of rules, or between a pair of lexical items. For example, let us consider a language with verb-final word order. Let us suppose that constructions with the verb not at the end but in middle position occur in discourse, because of pragmatic factors, imperfect acquisition, or some other kind of idiosyncrasy. Initially, these variants may be extremely rare and probably restricted to just one person. As we have seen, the learner performs an error-minimizing procedure in which he minimizes the discrepancy between his linguistic system and those he experiences. Faced with a majority form used by most of his peer group most of the time (verb-finality), and a minority form used rarely (verb-mediality), it will always be more accurate for the learner to acquire the majority form.

This is the *threshold problem*: when variants first arise, they are too rare to be learnt by new speakers coming into the community, who will always opt for the most common form. Even if sub-populations became isolated from each other, divergence in discrete variables would never occur, as each new learner's 'cleaning up' of the language input would return the grammar to its initial state.

Of course, my example is simplistic. What presumably happens in reality is that new learners would acquire verb-finality as the default, but also acquire a rule to the effect that the verb can be shifted to medial position under certain conditions. If other cues to case assignment were available, then learners might simply infer that word order was free. None the less, the problem remains that, at some point in time, certain variants are so rare as to be impossible to acquire. The learner might experience tokens of verb-medial constructions in certain contexts; but then he would have many more examples of verb-final constructions in that context. Since learners seem predisposed against acquiring several structures that do the same thing (Clark 1993), the strategy that brings the best match to the available data is to ignore the verb-medial variant.

The averaging and threshold problems seem to be quite general, and present a real challenge to our understanding of how languages can change.[3] There are certain classes of linguistic change that seem able to escape them. These are variables where the pattern of variation is skewed in a particular direction. For example, in discourse, the length of many words is reduced—final consonants are unreleased or omitted, and unstressed vowels are left out. There is no lower limit on the length of the phonetic token; where the word is contextually highly redundant, it may be reduced almost to nothing (Lieberman 1963). There is thus variation between the full form and truncated forms. However, forms *longer* than the full form never occur. The maximum length possible, given that speakers do not generally invent extra phonetic material and add it, is the fully articulated canonical form. A learner is thus faced with a range of variation between the full form and highly reduced forms. In this case, the variation encountered does not sum to zero, but is skewed towards reduction. There is, therefore, no averaging problem. The learner may still acquire the full form, because that is what he has encountered where the effects of coarticulation and context are slight. However,

---

[3] This is true as long as we assume that the learner's task is to match her output to the speech input in some (perhaps biased) way. An alternative approach to acquisition suggests that the learner does not attempt to match output to input at all. Instead, she searches for a few basic cues which she uses to set the parameters of an innate Universal Grammar one way or another (Lightfoot 1997). If Lightfoot's view is correct, then the averaging and threshold problems may not be as significant as argued here. However, this position is far from convincingly demonstrated, and at best can only apply to a tiny subset of linguistic items (those that are innately parameterized, if any actually are).

he may well acquire a shortened form as his underlying representation, as this is closer to the 'average case' he has encountered. He will then in turn produce a range of variants from the new full form to even more reduced forms.

Skewed variation of this kind has clear implications for language change. As Lüdtke (1986) has argued, because of the processes just described, phonological changes to words can in general only shorten them or leave them the same length. On average, then, they will tend to shorten. There are countless historical examples of the truncation process at work.

If phonetic erosion is ubiquitous, we would expect that all words in all languages would by now have been reduced to monosyllables, with all the problems of homonymy that that would cause. This has not happened, and the explanation given by Lüdtke is that, whilst phonetic changes are always in the direction of truncation, other, non-phonetic forms of change can lead to longer words. If a word form has become so truncated as to lose its distinctiveness, speakers tend to expand it in some non-phonetic way. The word may be replaced by a longer alternative, or a periphrastic expression may be formed. This will then get fixed as a word. An example discussed by Keller (1994) is the French form *aujourd'hui*. It seems that, at a certain point, the French form for today, *hui*, was so reduced as to be insufficiently contrastive (cf. *ouïr* 'to hear', *oui* 'yes'), and speakers introduced a periphrastic phrase to get their meaning across (*au jour d'hui* 'on the day of today'). This phrase has been fused as a single word, and the process of phonetic erosion has no doubt begun again. Lüdtke's insight is that the processes of phonetic erosion, lexical or morphological expansion, and fusion constitute a cycle through which individual word forms move in one direction only.

The question relevant to our purposes is whether this cycle will lead to words in related languages diverging. I suspect that it will. Phonetic erosion can take several different forms. Furthermore, there are countless ways in which lexical or morphological expansion can occur. Which one of these (if any) actually takes hold is a product of the linguistic items available and the creativity of speakers in performance. In short, there are many possible paths around the cycle, each with a low probability of occurrence, and just which path is followed is almost certainly unpredictable in detail. This means that word forms in two isolated languages will become less similar with time due to this intrinsic process.

This conclusion might seem to validate the basic insight of glottochronology, which stated that the number of basic words in two languages that are unrecognizably different will increase a simple function of the time since separation. Assuming that the operation of Lütdke's cycle eventually leads to words being unrecognizable as related, then it provides a mechanism for glottochronogy's 'lexical clock', as long as we assume that words change at a constant rate. However, as we have seen, there is little justification for that assumption, especially in view of the effects of changing social factors and language admixture.

Where variation is directionally skewed, then, languages can be expected to change in that direction, and diverge over time. Cyclical, unidirectional processes may be quite common in language change. Grammatical markers such as the English future form *will* originate as concrete words in their own right, which are gradually bleached of meaning. They may then become attached to the verbs they modify, so they are just affixes rather than separate words; then ultimately, by erosion, they may disappear altogether to be replaced by some other concrete word from the lexicon. Many processes of morphological and syntactic change may follow such cycles of erosion, reduction, and replacement (Hopper 1990; Bybee *et al.* 1994).

However, there are also many linguistic variables—probably most phonological and grammatical changes, and some lexical ones—where variation is not skewed, but can occur in any direction.[4] The averaging and threshold problems thus apply. It is difficult to assess the importance of these problems. It is clear that, if language change is caused simply by random variation, the ultimate expectation is that all changes should get averaged out. This is a real challenge to the adequacy of the neutral model as a theory of language change in cases where variation can occur in any direction. If the rate of variation were high enough, its stochastic effects might be sufficient to cause permanent instability in language norms under certain conditions of population size and structure. In general, the larger the social networks learners have, the more severe the averaging and threshold problems become, because the learner is averaging over a greater number of different individuals.

A more promising avenue would be to enrich the capacities of the learner. In the neutral model, the learner is seen as a simple mechanism for acquiring whatever language is going on around it. If the learner were instead selectively biased, either towards certain kinds of linguistic variant, or towards certain individuals as linguistic models, then the averaging and threshold problems could be much more easily overcome. I will consider these two types of bias in Sections 2.4.1 and 2.4.2. As to whether the averaging and threshold problems are fatal to the neutral model, I consider that to be an empirical question, whose answer is likely to depend upon the exact conditions in which learning occurs. I will, therefore, address it in a more concrete and detailed way in Chapter 3. I now turn to the third area of difficulty with the neutral model, which concerns its amplifier of variation, geographical isolation.

---

[4] Though Croft (1990: 227–9) suggests that many more processes of grammatical change are unidirectional than is at first obvious. Instances of apparent change in both directions may, on this view, represent either cycles or combinations of distinct processes whose effects work in opposite directions.

2.3.3. The geographical-isolation assumption

Let us rerun the neutral account of divergence. Groups of people become isolated from each other, and, because they are isolated, the random innovations that arise in one location are not transmitted to any others. Consequently, over time, the languages drift further and further apart as innovations accumulate. There is no question that *if* there is a source of effectively random variation, and *if* the averaging and threshold problems are overcome, then, as long as there is complete geographical isolation, languages will diverge. However, where geographical isolation is incomplete, it is unclear that they will do so. This is because innovations arising in one sub-population will tend to diffuse to them all. The neutral model, to the extent to which it is adequate at all, can therefore explain divergence only where there is total isolation. The question of whether human societies whose languages diverge are in fact always geographically isolated from each other thus becomes a very important one.

As in the case of the mechanism of inheritance, there are important differences between the biological and linguistic cases with respect to geographical isolation. Human sub-populations can become genetically distinct even if their members encounter each other every day. This is because, to diffuse a genetic mutation, one has not just to meet a stranger but to mate with them. Thus all that is required for genetic diversification is that there is no actual interbreeding. This is what must explain the persistent genetic differences observed between European peoples who we know have been trading and working together for centuries; in general, they do not choose to interbreed very much (Barbujani and Sokal 1990). In the linguistic case, on the other hand, variants are acquired not just from parents but potentially from anyone one meets during the period of language acquisition. Any form of contact whatever between sub-populations, even of a much more fleeting kind than intermarriage, could in principle prevent linguistic divergence. The requirement of geographical isolation is thus apparently more stringent in the linguistic than the biological case.

Empirically, it is extremely debatable whether groups whose languages diverge are generally isolated to the relevant extent. In the past, anthropological theory tended to assume that every society or culture was basically isolated from its neighbours (Wolf 1992). This assumption was rooted in both theoretical and practical convenience, as well as a tendency to portray non-industrial societies as timeless and pristine.

Many anthropologists would now question whether the isolation between different cultural groups has normally been complete. Studies of ethnicity have stressed how individuals may have several ethnolinguistic models available to them and switch between them according to their circumstances—sometimes even within one sentence (Patterson 1975; Otite 1990; Myers-Scotton 1993). Even the San Bushmen of the Kalahari, who for decades were held out as an undisturbed remnant of stone-age life, are now argued to have formed part of regional economic and political systems involving neighbouring Bantu farmers for hundreds of years (Headland and Reid 1989; Solway and Lee 1990; Shott 1992 and dozens of references therein). This affects not just their economy, but their whole cultural system (Jolly 1996). However, it has not led to them losing their ethnolinguistic distinctiveness.

This is not an isolated example. Again and again, where anthropologists have re-examined the history of small-scale societies, they have found, not geographical isolation, but a history of contact, exchange, and mutual influence. One very relevant example comes from New Guinea. New Guinea is the most linguistically diverse island in the world, with over 1,000 indigenous languages spoken by distinct tribes. However, it is becoming clear that the trading networks that went between groups were both extensive and long-standing (Hays 1993). In a detailed study of one part of New Guinea, Roberts, Moore, and Romney (1995) found that at least as much of the distribution of material artefacts was explained by inter-group diffusion as is explained by intra-group contacts. Furthermore, there is considerable evidence of linguistic diffusion between New Guinea languages (Foley 1986: ch. 7; Ross 1994, 1996). This is hardly a picture of geographical isolation, and an explanation of the great linguistic diversity will have to look elsewhere, as Hays (1993: 148) concludes:

Put simply, the 'ethnic groups' of 'the [New Guinea] Highlands', 'fringe', and 'Lowlands' have long been engaged in numerous and wide-ranging networks of interaction, but the result has not been homogeneity or uniformity. Why not? . . . Of course, constraints imposed by the environment, climate and disease may be part of the answer as far as some traits . . . are concerned . . . but what about the rest? If it is people as much as 'Nature' that create, maintain, or ignore boundaries, we need to know how and why.

For examples of similar conclusions for other regions, see, on Asia: Hoffman (1984), Abu-Lughod (1989); on the Pacific: Kirch (1991); on Amazonia: Meggers (1982). Barth sums up the situation well in his famous work on ethnicity:

it is clear that [ethnic] boundaries persist despite a flow of personnel across them. In other words, categorical ethnic distinctions do not depend on an absence of mobility, contact and information, but do entail social processes of exclusion and incorporation whereby discrete categories are maintained *despite* changing participation and membership in the course of individual life histories.   (Barth 1969: 9–10)

This anthropological revisionism squares well with what we know from sociolinguistics, which has been largely concerned with urban situations and industrial societies. Sociolinguistics has shown that considerable stable linguistic diversity can persist *within* a single society, and that diversity does not necessarily lessen if increased access to standard variants is given to non-standard speakers. Black English dialects in Philadelphia, for example, are diverging from standard

US English despite four to eight hours of exposure per day through school and television (Labov, cited in Chambers 1995). Increasing contact between two varieties may even speed their divergence (Labov 1972), because, as well as shifting their speech towards those with whom they interact, speakers may shift it *away* if the circumstances of contact are unfavourable (Bourhis and Giles 1977).

The lesson of these empirical findings is as follows. Whilst geographical isolation may lead to diversity in language, there are cases where diversity is produced and maintained in its absence. This is obviously problematic for the neutral model. There are two non-mutually exclusive explanations for diversification despite inter-group contact.

On the one hand, it may be that partial isolation is sufficient. The interaction between New Guinea tribes is presumably much less frequent on a day-to-day basis than the contact within the tribe. The question is how much less it has to be for inter-tribe linguistic diversity to be maintained. If 10 per cent, or 20 per cent, or 50 per cent of all social encounters are across an ethnolinguistic boundary, can that boundary be maintained? Again, this is an empirical question that can only really be answered by looking at a concrete case in detail.

On the other hand, other mechanisms that amplify linguistic variation may be more important where geographical isolation is lacking. I will consider such mechanisms in Section 2.4.

2.3.4. Correlated changes

By the logic of the neutral model, the particular suite of changes that affects a given language should reflect no more than chance and history, since changes accrue by independent, random mutation-like processes. However, the comparative study of languages has shown that this is not the case. There are correlations amongst the development of different items of grammatical structure, and these patterns recur in languages of diverse origin. We have already seen, in Chapter 1, the example of vowel systems. A language having three vowels has /i/, /a/, and /u/; one with five has /i/, /e/, /a/, /o/, and /u/, and not any other of the hundreds of logically possible combinations of vowel items (Disner 1984; Lindbom 1986). To take another example that we will discuss further in Section 2.4.2, languages in which the Object precedes the Verb use morphological suffixes but never prefixes, whereas languages in which the Object follows the Verb may use either. Patterns such as these are the subject of the sub-field of linguistic typology (Greenberg 1966; Hawkins 1983; Comrie 1989; Croft 1990; Dryer 1991, 1992), and they can be shown to have recurred across many independent lineages in linguistic evolution. They can thus be interpreted only as the result of some kind of functional linkage between different items, such that change in one makes changes in some others more or less likely to become fixed. In the neutral model, as we have stated it thus far, there is no mechanism by which this could happen.

The neutral model, then, is beset with obvious difficulties as a theory of language change. In the next section I will present two ways in which it can be enriched, which may overcome these problems. Both of them rely on the idea that learners, rather than sampling all the linguistic input available to them, perform some kind of selection on what will contribute to their own linguistic norms. This selection might work in two ways. First, it might be done on the basis of the social value of particular variants. Secondly, it might be done on the basis of their functional or communicational value. I will consider each of these in turn.

2.4. Additional Amplifiers

2.4.1. Social selection

The idea of social selection is, briefly, that the learner does not just pick up all the linguistic activity going on around him or her, but instead homes in specifically on that of a target group. Social selection has, interestingly, been shown to occur in the acquisition of song by songbirds (Beecher *et al.* 1994). Birdsong shows 'dialectal' diversity that is in some ways intriguingly like that found in human language. A young male song sparrow will preferentially acquire the songs of other males who have successfully established a territory in the neighbourhood. The learner will ultimately need to establish a territory in this area himself in order to reproduce, and may gain by sounding like the previously successful males on the same site. Selecting the type of song to learn is thus directly related to his life opportunities.

A case can be made for the proposition that social selection occurs in human language. The idea had been prefigured by Saussure and Sapir, but Labov's (1963) classic account of dialects in Martha's Vineyard, a small island off the coast of the north-eastern United States, was perhaps the first sociolinguistic study to provide quantitative and unambiguous evidence. The island has a resident population, and a large transient population of holidaymakers. The tourists have such an impact locally that it cannot be argued that residents have no access to standard American English. However, local phonological peculiarities still persist. What Labov showed was that the strength of an individual's adoption of the local accent markers correlated with his attitude towards the two groups. The more Labov's subjects resented the outsiders, and felt that their lot lay with traditional island life, the more strongly they adopted the local accent. On the other hand, the more they felt that outsiders enriched the possibilities of life, the more standard was their speech. This seems to be a clear case where different speech models are available, and learners are choosing the one to adopt on the basis of how they see their future social alliances. Numerous subsequent sociolinguistic studies have confirmed this result (see e.g. Chambers 1995: ch. 2).

These results have led to the formulation of a general model of language acquisition based on social selection by LePage (1968: 192):

Each individual creates the systems for his verbal behaviour so that they shall resemble those of the group or groups with which from time to time he may wish to be identified, to the extent that

> (*a*) he can identify the groups,
> (*b*) he has the opportunity and ability to observe and analyse their behavioural systems,
> (*c*) his motivation is sufficiently strong to impel him to choose, and to adapt his behaviour accordingly,
> (*d*) he is still able to adapt his behaviour.

LePage's social model relies on an inherent source of variation in language on which social selection can operate, but, given that, it seems to provide a mechanism for the maintenance of diversity even in the absence of geographical isolation, as the learner actively chooses certain models out of all those available. Social selection plays a role very similar to that played by sexual selection in speciation; it allows groups inhabiting the same space to diverge by active processes of choice and identification. It is one way in which, to quote Hays' article on New Guinea, 'people as much as "Nature"' may create ethnolinguistic boundaries. Why people should want to do this is a challenging question, to which I return in Chapter 3.

Social selection is likely to be a key amplifier of variation. It is worth briefly considering the possibility that it is actually a source of variation too. At various points in history, people have deliberately invented words that set them apart from other people with whom they do not wish to identify. The importance of this kind of intentional creation is probably marginal; most linguistic changes and most linguistic variables are well below the level of conscious control. We also know that speakers who want to signal social distance will subconsciously increase the rate of production of linguistic variables that make their speech distinctive, just as those who want to signal solidarity will do the opposite (Bourhis and Giles 1977). Now it may be the case, that where there are no such variables, speakers subconsciously introduce them, by some kind of random innovation. It is very difficult to demonstrate that this routinely occurs, but, if it does, it explains why new social dialects arise so fast when new social networks are formed. It would also shed interesting light on the evolutionary significance of language diversity, to which I return in Chapter 3. At any rate, it is at least possible that social behaviour is an additional source of variation as well as an amplifier.

2.4.2. Functional selection

The final mechanism by which diversification may be produced in language is what I shall call functional selection. Examples of functional selection appear in Chapter 3, and in more detail in Chapter 7, and so I will present only the basic principles here. Functional selection again relies on inherent variation in language. The learner has access to a range of different variants, not just because he or she is normally exposed to numerous individuals, but also because the performance of any one individual is variable over time. The probability of adoption of those different variants may not be equal. Through social selection, as outlined above, some may be associated with more influential speakers than others, but there may also be inherent reasons for preferring one to another. To give some examples, phonological distinctions that are hard to hear may not be reliably picked up by the learner. This prevents languages ever developing an infinite number of phonological contrasts. Grammatical structures that generate sentences that are hard to parse or remember are unlikely to be learned, and so, where there are two competing variants available in a language, that which produces the lower processing load will tend to win out. Where there are two variant forms of the same word, that which is easiest to pronounce is presumably more likely to be adopted, because of the general least-effort principles of motor learning (Lindblom 1990).

This kind of unconscious selection between available variants by learners gives a powerful mechanism for language change. In fact, it is the exact counterpart in linguistic evolution of natural selection. In the biological case, some mutations are much better than others at getting themselves replicated because they help build animals that are better at survival and reproduction. Those variants multiply at the expense of less fit alternatives, leading to the adaptation of organisms to their environment. The linguistic process of functional selection is adaptive in an analogous way; languages become more and more efficient at being learned and used by speakers. As I mentioned in Chapter 1, the linguist Max Müller recognized this parallel between language change and evolution very soon after the publication of Darwin's *Origin of the Species* in 1859. Hermann Paul, too, invoked a process of functional selection as an agent for linguistic change: 'In the development of language customs, function plays the same role as that which Darwin attributed to it in organic nature: the greater or lesser usefulness of the resulting patterns is decisive for their preservation or extinction' (Paul 1880: 32).

There are interesting explanatory approaches to comparative and historical linguistics based on the notion of functional evolution, which we will examine in more detail in Chapter 7. Here it is necessary to consider just how functional selection could lead to diversity in language.

In the biological case, natural selection is likely to produce diversity because environments differ. Mutations leading to water conservation will be fitter in the desert than in the rainforest. Here again, there is a disanalogy between linguistics and biology. Different species exist in different ecological niches. That is, some make their living under the sea, some in the air, and so on. The multiplicity of niches is assured by the climatic diversity of the world, and further enhanced by the fact that species live off each other. New grasses provide niches for herbivores;

a new herbivore species provides a niche for new species of gut parasites, ticks, and dung beetles, and perhaps a new species of carnivores. As the herbivore evolves in response to these unwelcome developments, so all the parasites and predators must in turn adapt or die. Thus species are constantly providing new ecological niches for others to live in, and so evolution continues along multiple and unpredictable paths.

The linguistic case seems quite different. All human languages are systems of communication and information storage used by human communities. They become adapted to the cognitive and productive capacities of human beings, but these are the same for the whole species. In other words, there is no obvious parallel to the ecological diversity of the biological case.

Let us consider an example. Across languages, suffixing of morphological affixes is much more common than prefixing (with infixing, where morphological information is inserted into the middle of the stem, much rarer still). Cutler, Hawkins, and Gilligan (1985) explain this tendency as a result of functional selection. They argue that lexical stems must be processed before the information derived from any affixes attached to them is usable. It follows that 'in the computational process of determining the entire meaning of a word from its parts, the stem has computational priority over the affix' (Cutler *et al.* 1985: 748). Thus an order where the stem is presented before any affixes—which mirrors the order of cognitive processing—will be computationally superior to any other. Faced with several variants, speakers will tend to select those that are computationally optimal, which, in this case, means stem followed by affixes rather than the other way around. Languages will thus tend to evolve towards suffixation.

The suffixing preference presumably apples to the speakers in every human society, and so it follows that we should expect all human languages to settle on suffixes rather than prefixes, and never change further. Rather than explosive diversification, functional selection seems destined to produce uniformity and stasis.

This conclusion is not inescapable, however. We need to consider that functional evolution does not occur along a single dimension. The computational demands of processing word meaning may favour suffixing, but in a language where Heads generally precede their dependents, suffixation would increase the complexity of the generalizations that the learner must acquire (for derivational and inflectional affixes may be considered to be the Heads of the morphologically complex word). Where there is a tendency elsewhere in the system for Heads to come first (as in languages with VO order or prepositions), there may therefore be an opposing pressure from acquisition to retain prefixing. This accounts for the observed typological pattern; only suffixation is found in OV or postpositional languages, whereas for VO or prepositional languages the picture is mixed, with both prefixing and suffixing often found.

In general, many factors, such as ease of articulation, ease of perception, memory load, and ease of learning, exert pressures on the adoption of variants into a language, and they often pull in opposite directions. Particular languages thus evolve under *competing motivations* (Haiman 1983).[5] Of course, the argument might come back that, even given competing motivations, languages will tend towards uniformity rather than diversity, because, given enough time, every language will discover the same optimal compromise between the different motivations.

This argument can be overcome. Consider a many-dimensional space with every dimension representing a different linguistic parameter. Thus, one dimension might be the size of the phonological inventory, another, some aspect of constituent order, another the level of morphological complexity, and so on. Different languages can be seen as occupying points in this space. Each point in the space has a fitness value, representing the extent to which a language at that point in the space will be effective at being learned and used by speakers. Under functional selection, languages should be expected to evolve towards the points with the highest fitness values. The point is that, in such a complex space, there is unlikely to be just one optimum position to which one can smoothly ascend from anywhere in the space. Instead, there may be a number of positions that are locally optimal and onto which languages may settle. There are, for example, no doubt local optima where languages use case-marking and free word order, and others where languages use word-order conventions and no morphology.

However, here monogenesis poses a problem. I take it as probable that all human languages ultimately stem from a single ancestor.[6] How, then, did they get into the different local optima which they now inhabit? There are two possible answers.

The first is that small random changes, arising from random variation or social selection, are sufficient to push different languages off into different parts of the state space. For example, a language with rich case marking could undergo a

[5] The term 'motivation' is somewhat unfortunate as it has teleological overtones and implies consciousness on the part of the language user. Neither of these implications is desired; by motivation I merely mean a factor related to language use that may influence the evolution of structure. The term has, however, become standard in the literature and so I continue to use it here.

[6] This cannot be shown outright from any linguistic evidence; there has been far too much linguistic evolution in the meantime, and periodic attempts to identify traces of the world's *Ursprache* do not stand up methodologically. However, other types of evidence converge to suggest that monogenesis is a reasonable assumption. The evolution of language requires very specific biological changes, which are present in all human populations, and it is extremely implausible to suggest that these could have occurred in multiple, convergent ways. Also, all human populations are closely related. Interpretations of the genetic evidence that claim it demonstrates an origin of our species in a single population in Africa around 200,000 years ago (Cann *et al.* 1987) are perhaps overstated. However, the genetic evidence does point to a very small human population until perhaps 60,000 years ago, and a mitochondrial DNA coalescence date of around 140,000 years for all living humans (Relethford 1995). Palaeontological evidence also tends to support a dispersal of a single population 'out of Africa' in the late Pleistocene, rather than a more diffuse origin for modern humans (Lahr 1994, 1996), though it is fair to note that differing interpretations remain on this point (cf. Wolpoff 1989, 1996).

random phonological change that merges the two phonemes that happen to distinguish the endings of the two key cases. With case endings no longer serving to assign grammatical relations, the language could then go into a rapid succession of changes familiar from many European languages and involving increasingly fixed word order, the gradual loss of residual case endings, the evolution of new constructions exploiting word order, etc. A couple of hundred years later, the grammar of the language would inhabit a quite different region of typological space from its parents and sisters, all due to a small phonological change. In the evolutionary literature, complex state spaces with several local optima are said to have *basins of attraction*. That is, in our example, once the validity of the case-ending cue had been disrupted, the language had been pushed over a watershed and thereafter was drawn inevitably into the region of the space occupied by languages with fixed word order.

As we mentioned in Chapter 1, the total linguistic context acts as an *ecosystem* for any particular linguistic item. The linguistic fitness of the phoneme /ɛ/ obviously depends which other phonemes the language in question already has—if it already has /e/ and /æ/, /ɛ/ may have trouble being distinguished and reproduced. Similarly, a rule allowing relativization on the object of a sentence may be less fit in a language where there is a passive construction than one without, for, in a language with a passive, one can always produce an object relative clause by a passive transformation followed by relativization on the derived subject (see Section 7.2.1). Thus as soon as one small difference between languages arises, the fitness landscape of all future variants will be altered, and they may go spinning off down different trajectories. Sapir (1921/1970: 152) recognized the power of this kind of process: 'Languages can change at so many points of phonetics, morphology, and vocabulary that it is not surprising that once the linguistic community is broken it should slip off in different directions. If once the speech of a locality has begun to drift on its own account, it is practically certain to move further and further away from its linguistic fellows.'

The existence of multiple optima with different basins of attraction may be an explanation of how small differences between languages get turned into large ones. The initial differences between languages must be supplied by the sources and amplifiers of variation we have already discussed. It is thus a powerful supplement to the causes of linguistic diversity, rather than a primary cause in itself.

The second way in which functional selection might lead to increasing diversity in language would be if different non-linguistic contexts favoured particular types of linguistic change. This is an argument that has already been developed in the literature on birdsong dialects (Date and Lemon 1993). Birdsong appears to evolve by a process of functional selection: those syllables that are easiest to hear have the highest probability of being picked up and adopted by learners. However, the acoustic characteristics of different habitats are different. The syllables that transmit well in woodland are not those that transmit well in open savannah. There are, in other words, competing motivations that favour certain syllables and vary from place to place. The result is dialect boundaries that track ecological boundaries (Tubaro *et al.* 1993).

Birdsong is a long-distance call system whose function demands that it be salient at great distances. This is why subtle acoustic characteristics of the habitat can affect it. Language, on the other hand, is generally used in face-to-face inter-action in small groups (Dunbar *et al.* 1994), and so is not likely to be affected by physical characteristics of the habitat in the same way. There might be other ways in which the social context affects the type of structures adopted, though.

Correlations between linguistic structure and life style, social organization, and so on were often suggested by nineteenth- and early twentieth-century compara-tive linguists, but are very much out of favour today. There are good reasons for this; the nineteenth-century work was hopelessly *post hoc*, and lacked rigorous cross-linguistic testing. Furthermore, no really convincing mechanisms were ever proposed to explain how the social factors cited actually influenced language change. Most contemporary linguists would therefore agree with Kaye (1989: 48) that 'there is no correlation whatever between . . . any aspect of linguistic structure and the environment. Studying the structure of a language reveals absolutely nothing about either the people who speak it or the physical environ-ment in which they live.' However, this is more a statement of presuppositions than an empirical finding; to my knowledge it has never been tested with all the rigour of modern typological linguistic sampling and statistical methods. The contrary position is conceivably true: different settings or social structures might favour one functional motivation over another for various reasons. For example, I find it quite plausible to suggest that a lingua franca spoken over a vast area, or by many people who acquire it as a second language, should be more affected by simplificatory pressures than one spoken in a small and stable community. I will leave such possibilities aside for the time being, but return to them in Chapter 7.

2.5. Summary and Conclusions

In this chapter I have discussed the basic mechanisms thought to be responsible for change and diversification in language. In the simplest possible model of language change, the neutral model, small variations arise more or less randomly in linguistic norms. These are due to performance factors, imperfect learning, and possibly social behaviour. If sub-populations become geographically isolated, then different variations tend to build up in each one as time goes by, leading to ever-greater discrepancies between the languages.

It is unclear that the neutral model is an adequate account of language evolution, as several key problems with it arose in the discussion. These were the following:

1. Random non-directional changes in language might be expected to cancel or average out in the acquisition process. It is, therefore, unclear how random variation alone can lead to sustained diversification in language.
2. Diversification sometimes seems to occur in the absence of geographical isolation. This is difficult to account for with a neutral model.
3. The path of linguistic diversification is not in fact a random one, as the neutral model predicts. There are patterns of structural correlation in the world's languages that represent parallel evolution.

Problems 1 and 2 may or may not be insuperable for the neutral model; it depends upon the precise rates of mutation, population structure, and learning algorithm assumed. To evaluate these difficulties, then, we must move from general discussion to a concrete case, which I will set up in the next chapter by using a computer simulation. Problem 3 definitely requires enrichment of the neutral model.

It was suggested that two additional mechanisms could be incorporated into the model to overcome the three problems. They were social selection, and functional selection under competing motivations. I shall incorporate them into the simulation of the next chapter, to try to discover how much difference they make to the evolution of linguistic diversity. The non-quantitatively minded reader, or she who is hungry for more empirical meat, may wish to skip Chapter 3, and move straight into the discussion of language diversity in Chapter 4.

3 Language Evolution: Computer Simulations

Truth is more likely to emerge from error than from vagueness.

(T. H. Huxley)

3.1. Introduction

The review of the mechanisms of language evolution in the previous chapter left a number of unanswered empirical questions. First, it is not clear whether the averaging and threshold problems can be overcome in groups of a realistic size. Secondly, it is unclear whether the neutral model can account for the finding that linguistic boundaries can develop and persist in the absence of complete isolation. Thirdly, the neutral model does not predict that changes will be correlated in the history of languages. Introducing social and functional selection to the model may or may not overcome these problems and provide a model that predicts sustained but systematic diversification. In this chapter I use computer simulations to suggest some more concrete solutions to these issues. As one of the main results of the simulations concerns the importance and power of social selection, I conclude the chapter with a discussion of the nature and function of that mechanism.

3.2. The Use of Computer Simulations

The optimal approach faced with these questions would be to design an experiment in which people learned language under various circumstances. We would record all the input they are exposed to, and test whether their acquisition was indiscriminate, or biased according to social or functional criteria. There would be various conditions of group size and group isolation. The amount of variation in speech would be measured, as would the rate of linguistic diversification resulting.

Unfortunately, for the social sciences (and sciences that study whole behaving organisms in general), the most interesting experiments are impossible to perform.[1] We are then left with two methodological choices. The first is to look

---

[1] This is not true of animals with a relatively short life cycle such as birds. Experiments with song-

for natural experiments; that is, to find several populations or groups that differ only on some parameter of interest, such as geographical isolation, and compare the linguistic outcome. Naturalistic studies have, for obvious reasons, been the backbone of the human sciences. They have been put to excellent effect by sociolinguists in the tradition of careful, quantitative study of language transmission pioneered by Labov (1963; see Milroy 1980; Chambers 1995). The results of these studies suggest the fundamental importance of social selection in language evolution.

Naturalistic studies have their limitations, however. Nature does not furnish us with the precise conditions we require. It is difficult to find clear enough matched populations to unequivocally assess the effect of any one variable. The time cost of getting data in a real human community is very large, and getting enough data to understand the general nature of processes is simply not possible in many instances, especially where the questions are of the 'what if?' variety.

This is where an auxiliary method may be of interest. That method is the use of mathematical or computer simulations. This has become widespread in evolutionary biology (see e.g. Sigmund 1995), as researchers have realized that facts about the general nature of evolutionary processes could be demonstrated in less than the (possibly infinite) time required for the right natural experiments to be identified and performed.

Computer simulations involve making a simple set of assumptions about how a process works (such as the various models discussed in the previous chapter), then implementing that process in a population of idealized organisms. These then live, die, and perform the relevant behaviours for varying lengths of time, and the outcome is measured in terms of the variable of interest. The conditions under which the idealized organisms operate can be varied, to provide a virtual experiment.

The value of simulations is clearly much less than that of genuine experiments. The organisms involved are very simple and not particularly realistic. They typically have very few possible behaviours and a simplified spatial world. The results of simulations can therefore rarely be considered as precise empirical predictions. On the other hand, a simulation is a great advance over a purely verbal argument. This is because simple processes at the level of the individual, particularly those with an element of randomness, can have quite unlooked-for emergent consequences in a population. Furthermore, a process that sounds reasonable verbally might not actually work when implemented, or only under very particular conditions. As we have seen, the arguments about the adequacy of the neutral model cannot be resolved by verbal means alone. Some kind of more concrete instantiation of language evolution is required at least to suggest the general effects of

birds have taught us a great deal about the transmission of song dialects (Beecher *et al.* 1994). Obviously, the difficulties in the human case are as much ethical as practical.

different factors, and the boundary conditions within which they work. It is in this spirit that the present simulation should be taken.[2]

Computer simulations have come to be used a great deal in the investigation of the evolution of communication (e.g. Levin 1994; Wheeler and Debourcier 1995), and have begun to appear in linguistics proper (Hurford 1987, 1989, 1991; Kirby 1993, 1995, 1998). There is only one study I know of which directly addresses the problem of how linguistic diversity arises.

In that study, by Jules Levin (unpublished, reported in Keller 1994: 100–5), there is a grid of 55 × 55 cells, each of which can be thought of as an individual or a village. There are two linguistic variants, A and A', and each cell is initially assigned one or the other at random. Thereafter, cells may change their variant to be like those around them. If the majority of their neighbours have A, they will change to A with a certain probability.

The simulation stabilizes with several homogeneous regions of A and several homogeneous regions of A', whose spatial distribution is described by Keller (1994: 101) as 'bafflingly similar to a map of isoglosses'. Levin concludes that '[language change may] be understandable on a grand scale as a kind of dynamic pattern emerging from simple interactive principles' (quoted in Keller 1994: 101).

This simulation is very interesting. However, it does not shed much light on the origin of diversity. The simulation begins in an artificially diverse state; that is, every cell is assigned a variant at random. Diversity only ever decreases in such a simulation, as one would expect, given that the 'speakers' just follow the maxim 'speak like your neighbours'. My present purpose, therefore, is to provide a more sophisticated simulation that begins with homogeneity and incorporates the various diversifying mechanisms discussed in Chapter 2.

3.3. Methods

In this simulation, the population lives on a spatial grid of 7 × 7 positions. At each location there is a group of individuals, which can be identified by its spatial co-ordinates. Thus, the group {1,1} is all the individuals living at the leftmost and

[2] A more powerful tool than computer simulation in these situations is analytical modelling of the type common in population genetics. Such models have been developed for the evolution of culturally-transmitted norms, of which linguistic items are an example (Cavalli-Sforza and Feldman 1981; Boyd and Richerson 1985). These models have the advantage of providing general, deductive solutions to questions about the outcome of particular evolutionary situations. With simulations, on the other hand, there is always a possibility that the results obtained are good for only the precise configuration of parameters simulated. However, simulation is a much easier technique to apply when dealing with populations that are finite, spatially structured, and not at equilibrium. Such populations are of interest in the current context. That said, there is much in the analytical framework of Boyd and Richerson (1985) that might be used to reinforce the arguments presented here. Social and functional selection appears in their models as 'indirect' and 'direct' bias, respectively, and they derive some general consequences of these biases. The threshold problem is partly indicated in their discussion of 'conformist selection'.

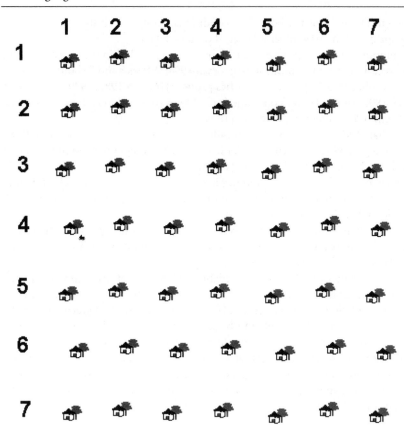

FIGURE 3.1. The 7×7 grid of the simulation

highest position on the grid (see Figure 3.1). There are twenty individuals in each group. This is in the range of the average hunter-gatherer band, which has been taken as a basic unit of coresidence by anthropologists for various purposes (Dunbar 1993: 684; Foley and Fitzgerald 1996: 541). The individuals have an age of between 1 and 5. After the fifth life stage, they die, and a new generation is born, such that the population size never changes. In each group there are four individuals from each age class.

Newborn individuals learn 'linguistic' structures from those around them. After the first life stage, however, there is no further learning, even if individuals migrate or the language changes. I thus assume a strict critical period for the learning of language. Though the validity of the critical-period concept remains subject to some disagreement, it is assumed by much linguistic theory to be a

TABLE 3.1. *The starting phonemes and their first- and second-formant frequencies*

Phoneme	Value	First formant (Hz)	Second formant[a] (Hz)
1	i	299	219
2	e	364	226
3	ɛ	481	198
4	ɑ	750	125
5	ə	377	140
6	u	290	63
7	o	392	69
8	ɔ	502	79

[a] The second-formant frequencies have been divided by ten.

central characteristic of the language faculty (Hurford 1991), and so it seems reasonable to include it in the simulation.

The only source of variation in the simulation is imperfect learning. I have not incorporated variation in performance. This a significant simplification. However, the two sources both have the same effect on the learner: they expose him to heterogeneity in the input. Imperfect learning is perhaps a more powerful source of change, as variants arising through it will be characteristic of an individual and repeated throughout her life. In contrast, many performance-related variants will occur only once owing to unrepeatable contextual factors. We can thus proceed, with the caveat that one rather enduring source of variation has been made to stand for two different sources, one enduring and one fleeting.

There are two types of linguistic item that we might consider, those that vary continuously and those whose variants are discrete. The phonetic value of a vowel segment, for example, varies continuously. Many other linguistic items require a discrete choice between two or more grammatical or lexical alternatives (Weinreich *et al.* 1968: 108). For the sake of clarity in the present simulation, I have chosen to restrict my attention to continuously variable items. In Section 3.8 I consider how the observed patterns may apply to discrete ones. As the reader will see from that section, the choice of continuous items for my simulations is not a fudge; my conclusions—that the averaging and threshold problems are significant, and that social selection must be very important in language diversification—are if anything more strongly borne out with discrete traits than continuous ones.

As my set of evolving linguistic items, I have taken the classic case of a vowel system. There are eight vowels, each defined by its first and second formant frequency in hertz. The starting values of the frequencies are from Javanese, which

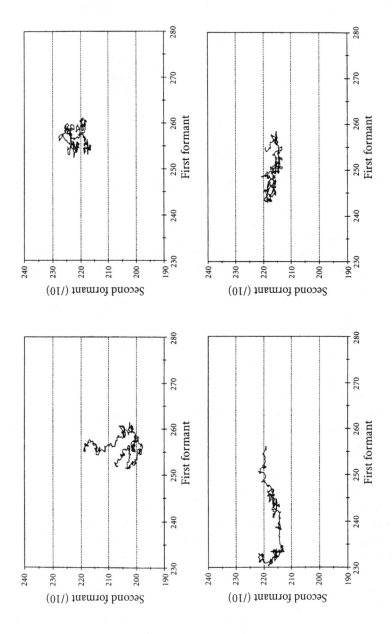

FIGURE 3.2. The trajectory in phonetic space of the group mean of phoneme 1 over 1,000 life stages of one group, for four different runs of the continuous simulation with NOISERATE = 2

has a very standard vowel inventory [i e ɛ ɑ ə u o ɔ] (Lindblom 1986: 32, frequencies taken from p. 7). These starting frequencies are shown in Table 3.1. The second-formant frequency has been divided by ten for ease of computation and to keep all the values in the same range.

An individual learns by sampling all the adults in its social group (that is, the adults from amongst the nineteen others at the same position on the grid). The phonetic targets that it adopts are simply the averages of those it samples. However, there is a noise parameter (NOISERATE). The final value adopted is altered (either increased or decreased, at random) by a random number between 0 and NOISERATE. With NOISERATE = 0, then, the individual simply learns the average value within its social network. Otherwise, its value departs a little at random from the norm. This is the basic program. Social selection and functional selection can be built in at a later stage.

In the basic social structure, all groups start with the same linguistic variables. There is no subsequent contact or communication between the groups. In other words, the basic case is that of a population dispersing in small bands that become totally geographically isolated from each other immediately after the dispersal. I will present some results from the simulations using this social structure, and then add in more realistic assumptions about inter-group contact, and then social and functional selection.

3.4. Basic Results

When the simulation is run with a non-zero NOISERATE, the values of the phonemes execute a random walk through phonetic space over time. The average of the frequencies used by the twenty individuals in one group for phoneme 1 is shown in Figure 3.2. Each run of the simulation produces a different trajectory, and the trajectories never repeat. The larger the value of NOISERATE, the further and more quickly the phoneme trajectory wanders from the origin (Figure 3.3).

As the phoneme values for each group are changing separately in this random fashion, considerable differences can emerge between the average phoneme values for one group and those for another group. This can be seen clearly by calculating the average formant frequencies for one of the phonemes in each of the forty-nine groups after 100 life stages of the simulation (Figure 3.4).There are clearly differences between the groups. It is necessary to try to quantify the strength of these to establish whether they constitute something like local dialects.

In order to do this, we need to consider not the absolute magnitude of the phonetic differences, but the locus of variation. In other words, the relevant question is whether individuals of group A differ from individuals of group B significantly more than they differ from each other. If they do, then distinct local norms have emerged.

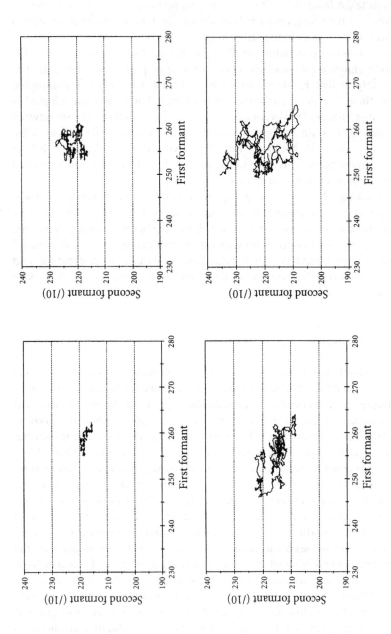

FIGURE 3.3. The trajectory of phoneme 1 in phonetic space over 1,000 life stages of one group for four runs of the continuous simulation with different NOISERATES: 1 (top left), 2 (top right), 3 (bottom left), 4 (bottom right)

	1	2	3	4	5	6	7
1	{256,220}	{255,218}	{257,215}	{259,219}	{253,216}	{257,224}	{249,219}
2	{252,218}	{250,218}	{259,222}	{252,217}	{256,221}	{255,220}	{257,217}
3	{260,219}	{255,220}	{254,215}	{247,220}	{254,218}	{255,216}	{253,221}
4	{255,221}	{257,222}	{257,218}	{252,219}	{257,219}	{254,218}	{258,218}
5	{250,218}	{259,218}	{253,219}	{252,219}	{255,223}	{252,220}	{256,218}
6	{258,217}	{253,222}	{259,222}	{259,222}	{261,216}	{256,218}	{256,214}
7	{256,216}	{258,217}	{258,221}	{257,215}	{254,220}	{256,218}	{254,218}

FIGURE 3.4. The average formant frequencies for phoneme 1 for the forty-nine groups after 100 life stages of the continuous simulation (NOISERATE=2)
Note: The common starting point was {255,219}

To measure local divergence, I have taken the frequencies for the first formant of phoneme 1 for all twenty individuals in four different groups. The groups are {2,2}, {2,6}, {6,2}, and {6,6}. An analysis of variance (ANOVA) was performed on these eighty frequencies. This procedure compares the amount of variation found within each group with that found between the groups, and provides a test statistic, the F-ratio, for assessing the statistical significance of any differences found. The larger the F-ratio, the greater the between-group differences relative to the within-group ones. The critical value for F to be significant at the 1 per cent level in the current case (3 and 76 degrees of freedom) is 26.22. That is, if F exceeds 26.22, then there are highly significant differences between the four groups.

Figure 3.5 shows the value of the F-ratio at the end of each life stage as the simulation progresses, for four different values of NOISERATE. It is clear that, even with NOISERATE set at just 1, highly significant inter-group differences have emerged by the 100th life stage. Although the exact trajectory of the F-ratio varies from run to run, significant differences always emerge with a non-zero NOISE-RATE. The F-ratio does not increase indefinitely; it ultimately levels out at a value determined by the NOISERATE, always well above the critical value (Figure 3.6).

The results of these runs are clear. Although random noise is ultimately expected to be self-cancelling, it can lead to significant local differences where groups are small and totally isolated. This is because the random output of one generation's learning gets fed into the next, providing a rather chaotic stochastic process. Having larger groups would obviously dilute the effect of stochastic variation, but, for a group size of twenty, a very small NOISERATE is sufficient to produce distinctive local dialects.

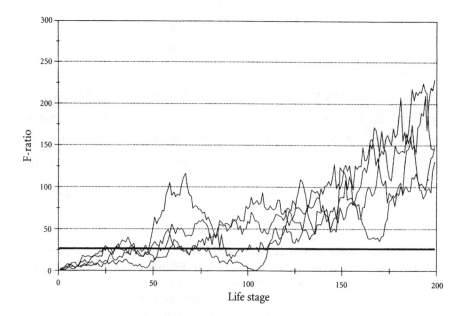

FIGURE 3.5. The development of the F-ratio over time for four runs of the simulation with NOISERATES of 1, 2, 3, and 4
Note: The thick horizontal line is the critical value for inter-group differences to be significant at the 1% level.

3.5. More Realistic Social Structures

Perhaps the most fundamental vector for inter-group diffusion is the permanent transfer of individuals from one group to another. The effects of such migration are added into the simulation as follows. After its first life stage, an individual may, with a probability given by a parameter MIGRATE, move permanently to another group chosen at random on the grid. For ease of calculation and to keep groups all the same size, an individual of the same age from the host group goes to the out-migrant's group of origin. In other words, they simply swap places. As language learning has finished by this point, the individuals take their linguistic variables with them and contribute them to the norm of their new group.

One real-life process that is directly analogous to this procedure is exogamy. Local exogamy often occurs within language groups. However, there are many cases of sustained exogamy across language boundaries. In the north-west

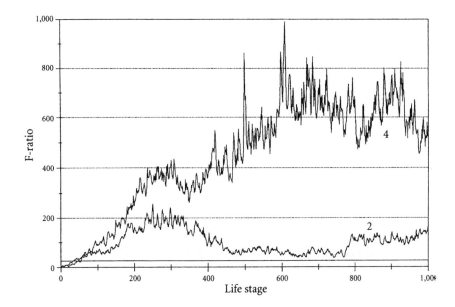

FIGURE 3.6. The long-term behaviour of the F-ratio, averaged over three runs of the simulation, for two different NOISERATES (2 and 4)

Amazon, for example, strict tribal exogamy has always meant that women marry into a different language group (Sorensen 1971, described in Hudson 1996). In such a tribe, the MIGRATE could be up to 50 per cent, if all the women out-married. Though the languages of the area show considerable grammatical convergence, they have persisted as clearly different, socially recognized systems with distinct lexicons. Linguistic diversity thus appears to have evolved despite the very high level of inter-group marriage.

Incorporating migration into the simulation drastically reduces inter-group differences. Figure 3.7 shows the development of the F-ratio with NOISERATE = 2 and either full exogamy (MIGRATE = 50 per cent) or partial exogamy (MIGRATE = 25 per cent). This latter rate works out on average at one individual leaving and joining each group of twenty per life stage. As is clear from the figure, the F-ratio never reaches the critical value for statistical significance. Distinctive local norms do not evolve.

More importantly, much lower migration rates are sufficient to prevent local diversity. Figure 3.8 shows the F-ratio for populations with no migration, and with MIGRATES of 1 per cent and 10 per cent (NOISERATE = 2). Even with the 1 per cent rate, which means on average one individual leaving a group every twenty-

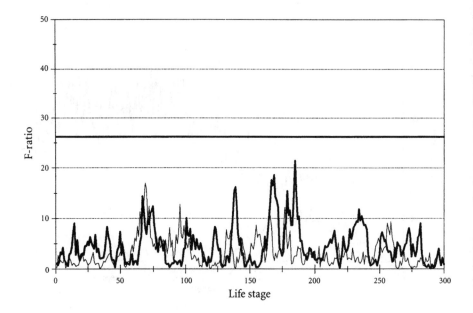

FIGURE 3.7. The F-ratio over 300 life stages for populations with partial exogamy
(MIGRATE = 25%) and total exogamy (MIGRATE = 50%)
Note: The critical value is never reached in either case.

five life stages, statistically significant inter-group differences are extremely intermittent. Increasing the NOISERATE makes little or no difference. This is
presumably because the F statistic is a *ratio*: it is affected by the proportion of
the variation that occurs between groups, rather than by the total amount of
variation.

The results of incorporating migration can be summarized as follows: even
small amounts of inter-group migration are sufficient to abolish diversity in the
continuous case. Linguistic diversity, it seems, cannot be very robust if it is based
on imperfect learning alone. In the next two sections I add in two mechanisms
that may make it more so: social selection and functional selection.

3.6. Social Selection

To incorporate social selection into the simulations, some individuals within each
group are assigned high status. This is assumed to be a product of non-linguistic
activities and is therefore done at random. Any individual has a 25 per cent

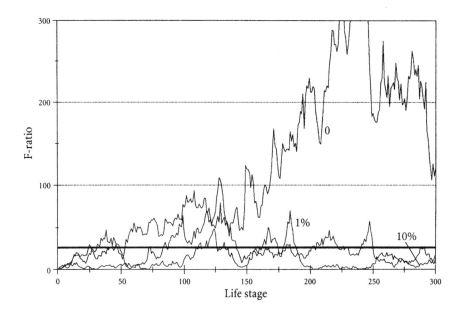

FIGURE 3.8. The F-ratio over 300 life stages for populations with no migration, MIGRATE = 1%, and MIGRATE = 10%

probability of acquiring high status at the end of the first age period, and it then keeps that status for life.[3]

In keeping with LePage's (1968) social model of language acquisition, learners do not use all the available linguistic models in acquiring the language. They instead incorporate only those with high status into the process, which then proceeds as before, with an imprecision specified by NOISERATE. In the event of there being no high-status individuals in a learner's group, the learner samples everyone as before. This arrangement corresponds to LePage's condition that social selection cannot take place unless the learner is able to identify and observe socially desirable models.

Including social selection greatly increases the F-ratios observed in the continuous simulation. Figure 3.9 shows the mean F-ratio over 300 life stages and five runs of the simulation for different values of MIGRATE for runs without social selection (line A) and with it (line B). The values with social selection are

---

[3] Sociolinguists would want to point out that there are social reasons for wanting to acquire a dialect other than it having high status. They distinguish dialects that are high in status from those that are high in solidarity—those that evoke local team spirit. In this simulation, I intend status as a more general construct, representing simply whatever it is that makes someone an attractive role model.

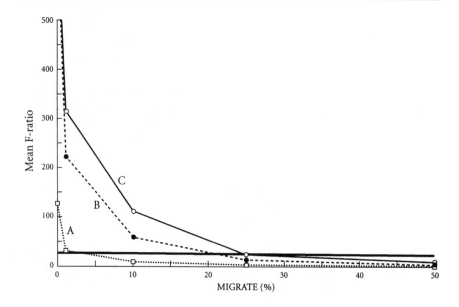

FIGURE 3.9. The mean F-ratio over 300 life stages and five runs of the simulation for populations without social selection (A), with social selection (B), and with social selection where migrants cannot transfer status (C)

significantly higher (pairing up runs of the simulation with the same NOISERATE, Wilcoxon matched-pairs test, $z = -4.37$, $n = 25$, $p < 0.001$). With social selection, a significant F-ratio is obtained with MIGRATES of 1 per cent and 10 per cent. Thus diversity is more robust faced with inter-group migration than when social selection is present.

When migrants move from group to group, they take their status values with them. We can also simulate a situation where in-migrants to a group cannot have high status. This may seem a rather *ad hoc* modification. However, social status in small-scale societies is often a product of being able to influence and mobilize networks of kin and friends, which a recent in-migrant by definition does not have. Incorporating the condition that migrants have low status in their new group seems likely to increase the robustness of local norms, as the migrant's language would not then normally be picked up by the next generation of learners.

Line C on Figure 3.9 shows the mean F-ratio for such a population. The F-ratios are higher than those obtained with ordinary social selection, but not significantly so (Wilcoxon matched-pairs test, $z = -1.84$, $n = 25$, n.s.).

These results clearly show how social selection by language learners can affect the evolution of norms. It reduces the amount of noise required in the learning process for local diversity to emerge, and greatly increases the robustness of that diversity against inter-group contact.

3.7. Functional Selection

The idea of functional selection is simply that some linguistic forms may be more readily adopted than others because they are easier to identify, learn, or use than the alternatives. Furthermore, the probability of one form being adopted will be contingent on which other forms are already present in the language. I will now incorporate some functional interaction between elements into the simulations.

The most famous example of functional interaction between phonemes is that vowels tend to be evenly distributed within the available phonetic space (Disner 1984). This can lead to the well-known cases of chain shifts: one phoneme moves into the phonetic vicinity of another, causing the latter to displace into the territory of a third, which then moves, and so on until all the vowel phonemes have been displaced one position in the phonetic space (Martinet 1955).

The mechanism by which such shifts are selected is presumably as follows. If, by random drift, two vowel phonemes A and B come to be very close in space, then learners will misinterpret the more extreme tokens of phoneme A as tokens of phoneme B. Their model of what constitutes phoneme A will then be skewed, as the end of the distribution nearest to phoneme B has been removed. They will thus acquire a version of phoneme A whose phonetic centre has been shifted away from phoneme B. This then spreads as a sound change that looks teleological; it is as if the language were 'trying' to keep its phonemes apart.

This kind of functional interaction between phonemes was incorporated in the following way. When a learner has been exposed to its linguistic input, the distances between the formant frequencies of all the average phonemes (after noise has been applied) are calculated. If the distance between any two phonemes is less than 10 Hz for the first formant or 3 Hz for the second formant, then one or the other phoneme is moved away until the critical distance is re-established. The phoneme to be moved is chosen at random.

To examine the effects of functional selection, we will follow the evolution of phoneme 7 instead of phoneme 1, as the former is much closer to its phonetic neighbours and therefore more likely to interact with them (the phonemes are defined in Table 3.1). Whereas, without functional selection, the formants just oscillate randomly around their initial values over time, with functional selection there are definite sound shifts caused by another phoneme pushing phoneme 7 out of its space (Figure 3.10). This is much more reminiscent of what happens in the history of real languages.

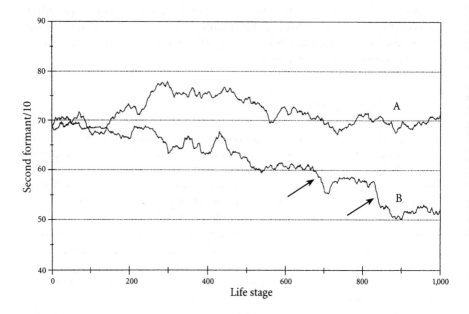

FIGURE 3.10. The mean second formant of phoneme 7 for one group without functional selection (A) and one with (B)

Note: The arrows indicate sound shifts.

Where there is no migration, functional selection greatly increases the mean F-ratio (Table 3.2). This is because sound shifts take small stochastic differences between dialects and amplify them into large systematic differences. However, where there is migration, the F-ratio is no greater with functional selection than without. Overall, the two conditions do not differ significantly (Wilcoxon matched-pairs test, $z = -1.32$, $n = 25$, n.s.). This is because sound shifts are always disrupted by migrants who do not have them.

Social and functional selection combined produce greater F-ratios than just functional selection, and the resulting diversity is robust against a MIGRATE of 10 per cent. However, these F-ratios are not significantly greater than those for the same phoneme for social selection alone (Wilcoxon matched-pairs test, $z = -0.74$, $n = 25$, n.s.). This may be because functional selection, as well as increasing inter-group differences, increases the within-group variance, as some individuals but not others adopt sound shifts. Thus, the overall ratio is no higher.

TABLE 3.2. *Mean F-ratio over 3,000 life stages and five runs of the simulation for the second formant of phoneme 7 with social and functional selection* (NOISERATE=2).

MIGRATE (%)	Selection			
	None	Functional	Social	Both
0	110.63[a]	229.60[a]	842.21[a]	460.30[a]
1	55.22[a]	43.44[a]	361.62[a]	361.72[a]
10	9.40	9.32	44.77[a]	50.56[a]
25	4.79	4.99	15.51	12.94
50	3.17	2.88	6.59	5.92

[a] $p < 0.01$.

3.8. Discrete Traits

In the above simulations we have considered only the evolution of continuously variable items. In this section I consider the similarities and differences that result if discrete variants are used instead.

I have presented a simulation very similar to the one described here, but with a discrete item, elsewhere (Nettle 1996a: ch. 2), and in a separate paper outlined a much more mathematically sophisticated simulation addressing a similar question (Nettle, forthcoming a). The learning algorithm used in the continuous case (leaving aside social and functional selection for the time being) is 'adopt the average of the variants being used around you'. The discrete equivalent is slightly different; it amounts to 'adopt the most common variant in use around you'.

Both the discrete simulations I have set out elsewhere show that most of the conclusions obtained with the continuous simulation apply equally to discrete items. That is, with no social selection, small amounts of inter-group contact are sufficient to abolish local diversity; social selection greatly increases the likelihood that distinct dialects or languages will evolve; and finally that functional selection influences the direction of divergence, and acts to amplify and reinforce diversity.

There is one major difference between the continuous and discrete cases. That is, in the discrete case, even with imperfect learning and no inter-group contact, local diversity is very difficult to evolve without social selection. The rates of imperfect learning have to exceed 20 per cent for diversification, or indeed any change at all, to occur in groups of twenty individuals (Nettle 1996a: 46–9). Thus diversity evolves much more easily when traits are continuous than when they are discrete. To see why this must be the case, one has only to consider the fate of variants in the two cases. In the continuous case, every random mutation contributes to the group mean, which is the starting point of the next generation's learning. In the discrete case, only the most common variant is expressed in what is acquired by the next generation; rare mutants are simply ignored. Thus local diversity cannot easily get established unless there are strong biases due to social selection (Nettle, forthcoming *a*).

3.9. Discussion

The results of the computer simulations may be summarized as follows.

1. Geographical isolation and noise in learning are sufficient to produce diversity in continuous variables. They are not sufficient to produce diversity in discrete variables unless the level of noise is set extremely high.

2. A very low level of inter-group contact, in the absence of social selection, destroys local diversity.

3. A mechanism of social selection hugely increases both the amount of diversity which evolves and its stability against inter-group contact.

4. Functional selection amongst the different variables in a language can amplify and reinforce diversity, though the initial diversity must stem from random noise and/or social selection.

These conclusions are obviously suggestive rather than demonstrated. The simulations, like any computer simulations, are simplistic in a number of ways. This is not a problem in itself, as we are not attempting to produce precise quantitative predictions, but rather to explore some general patterns. What is important is that none of the simplifications involved in writing a computer program falsify the general character of the processes under investigation.

There are several key simplifications in this simulation that should be mentioned. These are, first, that the variation on the items used is multi-directional, and secondly, that the competence of the organisms is homogeneous. Thirdly, the only type of inter-group contact allowed is permanent migration, and, fourthly, the functional interrelations between elements are very limited. I will briefly discuss each of these in turn.

The first simplification is that variation on the vowel formants simulated can occur equally in either direction. This means that the ultimate expectation must be no change and that random fluctuations should over the long run sum to zero. This puts vowel phonemes into the class of linguistic items to which the averaging and threshold problems apply. As we saw in Section 2.3.2, however, where variation on an item is skewed in one direction, then directional or cyclical change is expected and the averaging and threshold problems do not apply so strongly. What proportion of linguistic items have skewed variation is unclear, but the dynamics of linguistic evolution will be rather different for them than for the multidirectional items simulated here. The effects of inter-group migration and social selection may not, however, be very different.

The second simplification involved in my simulation is that the competence of my simulated organisms is homogeneous. Real human beings, in contrast, have access to not one but several speech styles that they may switch between according to the context. This may mean that they are bilingual, or simply that they command several dialects or registers. Thus human competence contains an orderly heterogeneity of different structures with different social values, rather than a single homogeneous grammar.

Failure to take this into account is not just a problem for my simulations. Grammatical theory in general has tended to ignore heterogeneity by referring to an 'idealised speaker-listener, in a completely homogeneous speech community' (Chomsky 1965: 3), much to the annoyance of some sociolinguists (Weinreich *et al.* 1968; Chambers 1995: 26–7). For this simulation, too, I feel it is acceptable to idealize away from heterogeneity. The main points of the simulation would be no different and probably even clearer if each individual learned several different norms appropriate to different contexts. Heterogeneity increases the possible speed of language change, as the variation present in coexistent dialects can quickly be converted into change if the social situation demands it.

The second simplification inherent in the simulations is that the only type of inter-group contact allowed is permanent migration. In reality, contact is much more often of a more fleeting kind, for example through trade or other economic interaction. However, this really does not make a great deal of difference. A MIGRATE of 10 per cent effectively means no more than that 10 per cent of the linguistic models for a learner are from outside the group. Those outsiders could be passing traders or seasonal visitors just as well as permanent migrants. I have also run simulations where there is short-term visiting between groups rather than permanent migration. This modification makes no difference to the principal finding that even a small degree of inter-group contact reduces or destroys diversity.

Finally, it is worth stressing that the functional interactions between linguistic elements in the simulations are very limited. In the continuous case, one vowel phoneme can affect the selection of another; in the discrete case, one grammatical parameter can affect another. In a real language, as well as numerous interactions within the phonology, syntax, and morphology, there are interactions *between* these levels. This may have particular implications for the finding that without social selection diversity can evolve plausibly only in continuous variables. In reality, diversity in a continuous variable such as the phonetic position of two vowel phonemes could lead to diversity in discrete parameters. To pick up an example I mentioned above, let us suppose there are two dialects that differ quantitatively, in the phonetic realization of the vowel phonemes. Two phonemes that drift near to each other in one dialect may be reanalysed as a single phoneme. Any morphological distinctions dependent on that phonological distinction may then in turn be lost, and some syntactic strategy may be selected to compensate, and soon there will be systematic discrete differences between the dialects at all levels, as a simple result of stochastic continuous differences. The functional mechanism may therefore be much more powerful than it appears here.

As long as these limitations are borne in mind, I feel these results are interesting and suggestive. If they have any implications for reality at all, they are as follows. There must be an inherent source of linguistic variation in language, stemming from acquisition or performance. However, this is not a sufficient condition for linguistic evolution. Both the social and functional selection mechanisms must be operating on this variation. The functional mechanism must be at work because it produces lawlike phenomena like chain shifts amongst phonemes, and universal co-occurrence patterns amongst grammatical items. If there were no functional selection, then different grammatical characteristics would be randomly distributed amongst the world's languages, which is not the case. The social mechanism must be at work because it is much the most powerful way of generating and maintaining diversity, even in the simplistic form in which it is implemented here. Indeed, it seems that only social selection could explain the situation in areas like the New Guinea Highlands, where great linguistic diversity has evolved despite significant inter-group contact. In the concluding section of this chapter I discuss possible reasons why social selection could have come to be so important.

3.10. Adaptive Significance of Social Selection

The simulations have suggested that a key force driving the relentless diversification of languages is the active selection by speakers of particular linguistic norms for social reasons. This suggests, from a theoretical perspective, something that sociolinguists have been urging from empirical observations for several decades now: the fundamental importance of social factors to language evolution (Weinreich *et al.* 1968).

Most sociolinguistic studies have been carried out in Western urban populations, but the way a person speaks is a signal of his social identity in societies from every continent and historical epoch. African hunter-gatherers classify strangers according to their speech and react accordingly (Wiessner 1977; Woodburn 1986), and the Bible tells us how the Gileadites used dialect to identify their enemies the Ephraimites (Judg. 12: 4). Our skill in placing an individual into a regional or social category according to a short sample of speech is remarkable and often quite unconscious.

These considerations suggest that the use of language as a marker of social identity is an integral part of human language abilities. As Chambers (1995: 208) puts it: 'The fact that linguistic variability is universal and ubiquitous suggests strongly that it is fulfilling some essential human need.' Chambers (1995: 250) goes on to suggest that 'The underlying cause of sociolinguistic differences . . . is the human instinct to establish and maintain social identity'.

But why should there be such an 'instinct'? We have already seen how young songbirds choose their song models from the successful territory-holders in their area (Beecher *et al.* 1994). For them, there is a clear and direct pay-off in reproductive fitness from selecting the right dialect. What could be the equivalent pay-off for a human language-learner?

There is abundant experimental evidence from several societies that people are more disposed to cooperate with others who have the same dialect as themselves than those who have different dialects, even when dialectal differences are so slight that they do not impair comprehension (Feldman 1968; Gaertner and Bickman 1971; Harris and Bardin 1972; Giles *et al.* 1975; Lang 1992). Learners selecting the right dialect will thus enjoy greater social success in the groups to which they aspire to belong. This still leaves the question of why the established members of those groups should so prefer and reward dialectal conformity. This question goes beyond just language, and concerns the nature of human groups in general. Indeed, it goes well beyond the scope of this book, though I have briefly considered it elsewhere (Nettle and Dunbar 1997; Nettle, forthcoming *c*), and I will review some ideas on it here.

Given that writing is a recent and rather localized invention (television even more so), we might reasonably say that societies are typically nebulous sets of social alliances based on face-to-face interaction between individuals. Though conflict, deceit, and exploitation are undoubtedly universal, most human interactions, particularly within societies, are remarkably cooperative. Through language, individuals exchange useful information about the world, strike bargains, and organize joint ventures. Foods are bartered, gifts are given, favours are done. In this way, societies constitute impressive systems of mutual aid that allow people to solve socially problems that would defeat them alone. I will argue in the next chapter that such networks of mutual aid are vital in enabling people to survive in different ecosystems.

A considerable literature has grown up on the evolution of cooperation (Axelrod 1984; Axelrod and Dion 1988; Ridley 1996). The findings of this literature suggest that, whilst cooperation can clearly confer benefits on individuals, it is only under rather restricted circumstances that it can evolve by natural selection. This is because evolution favours the fittest individuals, and, in general, individuals who are trusting and honour their debts have lower fitness than those who exploit others, deceive them, and take all the benefits of society without paying the costs. The evolution of cooperating groups is thus disrupted by cheats or 'free-loaders' who drive the cooperators to extinction.

There are two ways in which cooperation can overcome the disruptive effects of selection for individualists. First, where individuals are close kin, they have an intrinsic interest in each other's survival, and so cooperation is more likely to be selected for. However, although kinship is of great importance to the structure of human social networks, cooperation extends far beyond close biological relatives in even the simplest societies. The evolutionary basis of human cooperation is therefore more likely to be found in the second mechanism, which is that of reciprocity.

Where individuals are likely to meet again many times, it may pay one to help the other, even at cost to himself, as the favour may be returned when the situation is reversed at a later date. Thus cooperation can evolve in a Darwinian universe of self-interested individuals as long as the probability of those individuals encountering each other repeatedly is very high (Axelrod 1984). Whilst this condition may be met in sessile organisms, in mobile organisms cooperation is more problematic, as anti-social individuals can constantly move around and find new victims to exploit (Enquist and Leimar 1993). As the size of the interacting group increases, too, the possibilities for cheats increase (Boyd and Richerson 1988). The prospects for the evolution of reciprocal cooperation in highly mobile savanna hominids living in large groups are thus fairly poor.

Yet our ancestors undoubtedly did evolve cooperative social systems. These systems do seem to be based on reciprocity, though of a very generalized kind in which trust and aid are extended to all others of the same social group with little bookkeeping or demand for immediate pay backs. According to Wiessner (1977: 98), the family of modern !Kung San hunter-gatherers 'surrounds itself with a community of others who will give assistance of any kind as they can, and place no demands on amount or timing of return except that in a reversed situation of have and have not, a return will be made'.

Our willingness to cooperate with others, even near strangers, persists, and indeed is the basis of more complex societies too. Caporael *et al.* (1989) provide experimental evidence that people are often quite willing to cooperate with strangers even in the absence of dependable pay-offs. This generosity and trust do not seem at first blush to be predicted by evolutionary theory. However, willingness to cooperate often extends only up to linguistically identifiable boundaries. Contrast the in-group generosity of the San with the fact that 'people, even San, of a different language group . . . are foreign people and to be regarded with suspicion' (Wiessner 1977: p. xix). The experimental studies cited by Caporael *et al.* involve appeals for assistance by members of the same linguistic group; many other studies, as I have already mentioned, show that having a disfavoured dialect greatly decreases the probability that cooperation will be successfully obtained.

If cooperating groups develop a distinctive speech form, and also insist on conformity to that speech form as a criterion of access to the social group, then cooperation is likely to be much more stable (Nettle and Dunbar 1997). This is because learning a dialect or language is difficult and quite lengthy. Any individual who has done it has therefore necessarily been interacting with members of that social group for a long time. Furthermore, having learnt the relevant speech form makes it much more difficult for any member to leave the group, as anywhere else he would be instantly recognizable by his speech as an outsider, and would have to begin, in so far as he was still able, the process of language learning again.

Social dialect is thus, in essence, an honest signal of group affiliation. Of course, today the situation is more complex, as individuals master many speech forms, and switch between them according to the circumstances, but this in no way undermines the idea that the origin of social selection was in a mechanism for signalling and enforcing cooperative group membership. Cooperation also occurs across language and dialect boundaries, of course, but again this does not contradict the idea that the strongest social bonds tend to involve linguistic conformity, or that in the absence of other information dialect is used in social assessment. This 'social-marking' theory, sketchy as it is, predicts the evolution of considerable skill in mimicking and assessing dialects, and a tendency to extend solidarity preferentially to individuals of similar speech to oneself. These are obvious characteristics of human language use. The social-marking theory also predicts that linguistic boundaries will form around the core networks of cooperation and exchange in which people are involved in their daily lives. Where individuals have large and dispersed social networks, we should expect linguistic uniformity over a wide area. Where social networks are small and tightly self-contained, many distinct languages will ultimately evolve. This prediction will prove of use in the next chapter, when we consider the spatial distribution of different languages across the globe.

4 Language Diversity: Patterns in Space

4.1. Introduction

In this chapter, we move on from the mechanisms that produce linguistic diversity in general to the actual distribution of languages in the world. I shall be trying to explain why there are so many, and why they are distributed the way that they are.

Defining and counting distinct languages is problematic, as it is far from clear exactly what constitutes one language. I shall return to this problem in Section 4.2. For the time being, we merely need to note that linguists do often refer to such entities, and furthermore that an impressive catalogue of the world's languages has been compiled by the Summer Institute of Linguists and published as the *Ethnologue* series (the most recent of which, at the time of writing, was Grimes 1993).

Grimes (1993) lists 6,528 distinct living languages, plus a number of extinct ones. A first observation about this number is that it is vastly greater than most people realize; non-specialists are hard pushed to name more than a couple of dozen languages, and estimate the global total in hundreds or tens rather than thousands. This is because the overwhelming majority of languages are spoken by small groups living in the Third World, as we shall see.

The second point to make about the languages in the *Ethnologue* concerns the unevenness of their distribution. The speakers of the ten most widely spoken languages add up to half the world's population.[1] On the other hand, there are literally thousands of very small languages, and these are much more numerous in some countries than in others, as the following examples clearly show.

Papua New Guinea, the small state in the Pacific that occupies somewhat more than half of the island of New Guinea, has 862 languages listed in the *Ethnologue*. This is 13.2 per cent of the languages in the world, yet Papua New Guinea's population of under 4 million represents only 0.1 per cent of the world population, and the country comprises only 0.4 per cent of the world's land.[2] Cameroon, in West Africa, has 4.2 per cent of the world's languages (which is 275 languages),

---

[1] The speakers of Chinese, English, Spanish, Hindi, Portuguese, Bengali, Russian, French, Japanese, and German add up to approximately 2,633 million, though this calculation is slightly problematic, since many of the speakers of these languages are bilinguals whose primary language at home is something else.

[2] The population and land-area percentages are calculated from figures in World Bank (1995).

0.2 per cent of the population, and 0.4 per cent of the land area. At the other extreme, China has 2.6 per cent of the languages, 21.5 per cent of the population, and 8.6 per cent of the land area, and Russia has 1.5 per cent of the languages, 2.8 per cent of the people, and 15.3 per cent of the land.

We can obtain a better overall impression of the global distribution of languages by mapping it. In Figure 4.1 countries are shaded according to their relative language diversity. For every country larger than 50,000 km², the (logged) number of languages spoken and listed in the *Ethnologue* has been regressed against the (logged) area of the country. The country has then been shaded according to the value of the standardized residual. The darker the shading, the more relatively linguistically diverse the country. Note that the resolution of the map is only at the level of the country—countries such as India and Mexico that have very diverse and less diverse regions are shaded uniformly according to the country-wide average.

Several clear patterns can be observed in Figure 4.1. First, language diversity tends to be greatest near the equator and decrease as one moves north or south away from it, as several authors have noted (Nichols 1990, 1992; Breton 1991; Mace and Pagel 1995). Species diversity decreases in a similar way as one moves away from the equator (Stevens 1989; Mace and Pagel 1995).

Secondly, there are more specific associations between language and biological diversity. In the Old World, there are two great belts of very high language diversity, which correspond almost exactly to the two great belts of equatorial forest that harbour so many of the Old World's species. One runs from the Ivory Coast across West Africa into Zaire. The other runs from south India and peninsular south-east Asia down through the Indonesian islands into New Guinea and the islands of the western Pacific. I have no estimate of the proportion of the world's species whose ranges are found within these two areas, but totalling up the languages given in the *Ethnologue* for the seventeen main countries involved[3] gives 3,929, which is 60 per cent of all those in the world.[4] These seventeen countries represent 27 per cent of the population and just 9 per cent of the world's land, yet they are home to three out of every five languages. As well as being plentiful where species are numerous, languages are few where species are few. Large areas of white on Figure 4.1 correspond to the Sahara and Arabian deserts and the plains of Central Asia, which though in the tropics are arid and poor in species.

Thirdly, the New World distribution is slightly different from that of the Old World. There is a latitudinal pattern, but the highest diversity is not in Amazonia,

---

[3] The Ivory Coast, Ghana, Togo, Benin, Nigeria, Cameroon, Zaire, Tanzania, India, Vietnam, Laos, Phillipines, Malaysia, Indonesia, Papua New Guinea, Vanuatu, and the Solomon Islands.

[4] This number will be very slightly inaccurate, as languages spoken in two neighbouring countries will have been counted twice. This probably involves no more than thirty or forty languages in a total of nearly 4,000.

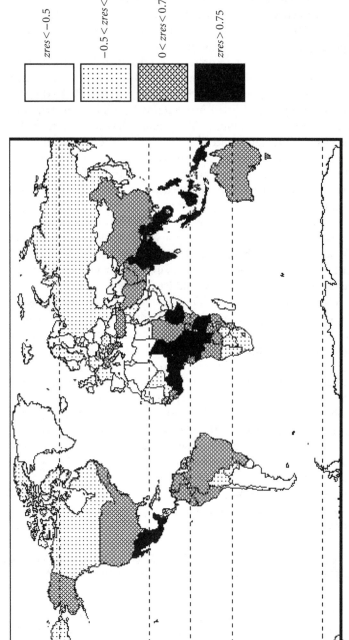

zres < −0.5

−0.5 < zres < 0

0 < zres < 0.75

zres > 0.75

FIGURE 4.1. Map of the world showing the relative language diversity of the major countries.
Note: Language diversity is calculated by regressing the logarithm of the number of
languages spoken in the country against the logarithm of the area of the country, and
shading each country according to the value of the standardized residual.
Source: Nettle (1998*b*), by courtesy of Academic Press.

as we might expect, but in Mexico. Furthermore, the overall level of diversity is lower than in the Old World. I will discuss possible reasons for this in Section 4.7.

None of these three patterns is a simple product of there being more people in the more diverse areas, as I shall show in Section 4.7. The orders of magnitude of the differences are also very large. We have, therefore, some strong trends to explain: language diversity is inversely related to latitude, is low in deserts and arid places, is high in the environment that produces equatorial forest, and is relatively low and anomalously distributed in the New World. The purpose of this chapter, then, will be to try to explain these trends. Before doing so, however, it is necessary briefly to examine the basis on which languages are identified and counted in studies such as this one.

4.2. Quantifying Language Diversity

The foregoing discussion has simply adopted uncritically the lists of languages provided by the *Ethnologue*. Reliable lists of languages can be made only where there is a clear way of deciding when two speech forms are different languages and when they merely constitute varieties or dialects of the same one.

The distinction between language and dialect is often made using social considerations as well as linguistic ones (Romaine 1994: ch. 1; Campbell 1998: 193–4). The folk usage of the distinction is a social one, based on identifying 'those speech varieties that belong to our wider group of people' versus 'those varieties that are foreign'. The linguists' definition is based on the criterion of mutual intelligibility, and formal techniques have been devised for measuring this (Casad 1974). However, not only are these techniques rarely used in the field, but their very basis is problematic. First, intelligibility is a graded phenomenon, and there can be various degrees of partial understanding. One may find chains of speech forms in which all neighbouring varieties are mutually intelligible, but those at the opposite ends of the chain are clearly not. It is not evident how the boundaries should be drawn in these cases. Secondly, mutual intelligibility can be asymmetrical, with group A able to understand group B but not vice versa. Thirdly, intelligibility varies a great deal according to the context and the particular speakers involved, and, fourthly, intelligibility depends on how much the parties involved want to understand each other, which is a product not of linguistic structure but of local social factors (Wolff 1959; Hudson 1996: 35–6). Thus the linguist cannot, in some cases, free himself entirely from social considerations in drawing the boundaries.

These difficulties have led some authors to suggest the abandonment of the use of 'language' as a technical term that individuates a particular speech system (Hudson 1996: 36), unless in the Chomskyan sense of 'I-language', which is the linguistic knowledge in the brain of a single speaker (Chomsky 1986).

I believe we can accept the indeterminacy of the language concept without having to disregard as worthless data such as that provided by the *Ethnologue*. I will argue this case, again, by pointing out the instructive parallel with the concept of biological species.

Species are sometimes individuated by biologists using the criterion of (in)ability to interbreed in rather the same way that linguists use mutual (un)intelligibility. However, here again, there are problematic cases (Abruzzi 1982). There are partially successful forms of interbreeding, and we will draw the boundaries differently if we count production of a zygote, birth of a live offspring (which would make horses and donkeys the same species), or fertility of that offspring (which would make them different species) as an example of success (Sokal and Crovello 1970). There are also chains, particularly in birds, where all neighbouring sub-populations can interbreed but those at the extremes of the chain cannot. This is most striking in 'ring' species, such as those of some gulls, where the chain goes all the way around the world, and the two sub-populations representing the ends of the chain actually live side-by-side as quite different species without interbreeding (Mayr 1963). Interbreeding can also be asymmetrical. In the bird species *pipiens*, the males of the south German variety can interbreed normally with females of other European varieties, whilst south German females have less than 1 per cent interfertility with other males (Mayr 1963: 42). Animal populations that could interbreed often fail to do so. Mallard and pintail ducks, like dogs and wolves, show complete interfertility in captivity, yet in the wild they do not choose to interbreed. This makes them different species, since what is crucial is not the physical possibility of interbreeding but its lack of occurrence in the natural population. I have not even touched on the difficulties of defining species in asexual organisms, where the interbreeding criterion is obviously absent.

Placing species boundaries, then, is much like placing language boundaries. It is not just a matter of using techniques to discover genetic discontinuities that are inherent in nature (Abruzzi 1982: 15). Though there are clear cases of well-defined species, there are also problem cases. Boundary placing typically involves making judgements about probable reproductive isolation or near-isolation on the basis of *ad hoc* sets of phenotypic characteristics, sometimes including behaviour. Despite this vagueness, the concept of species plays a key role in all the biological sciences, and ecologists regularly count species in order to arrive at generalizations about ecosystems.

I will argue that the language as a unit should likewise be saved for certain purposes, as long as we understand its limitations. Language boundaries, though they can be blurred, are often clear and sharp. Furthermore, people themselves tend to believe boundaries to be genuine and important in their lives. The ultimate justification for counting pintails and mallards as separate species is that, although they live in the same places, they do not choose to interbreed (Mayr

1963). Similarly, people perceive language boundaries, often accurately, and wish to maintain them. Though this is not an infallible guide to the underlying linguistics, it is certainly prima-facie evidence of real communicative discontinuities that we should try to identify. I will thus try to justify holding onto the language concept in the following ways.

First, the linguistic arbitrariness of the language/dialect criterion is relatively unimportant, as long as that criterion is employed approximately self-consistently. As long as this is the case, then counts of what are deemed to be languages will give a reasonable relative measure of diversity. Linguists seem to agree often enough in practice for this assumption to be made. The *Ethnologue* aspires to be based on the linguistic notion of language rather than a social one. However, given the lack of detailed scientific work on a large proportion of the world's languages, it must be acknowledged that local folk conceptions—which are socially based—must have played a large part in the database's construction. This is not a serious problem as long as there is a general correlation between socially identified boundaries and linguistic discontinuities. Common experience, as well as the considerations of Chapters 2 and 3, lead us to expect that this might be so, for, once a major social boundary is established, then linguistic norms will cease to be transmitted across it, and divergence will begin. Dixon (1997: 7–9) makes a similar argument; either mutual intelligibility between two varieties will stay very high, because there is communication across a boundary; or, if that communication ceases, intelligibility will quickly drop to near zero as complexes of changes accrue in the separate languages. The problem cases, of intermediate intelligibility, or of a major discrepancy between the social and linguistic boundaries, will be relatively rare and betoken some special circumstance such as the recent split or change in social organization of two communities.

Secondly, although error is introduced into our data by the indeterminacy of language boundaries, this error is effectively random. It is thus more likely to obscure real trends than create apparent ones, and any clear patterns that are still evident are likely to represent genuine effects. Thirdly, the orders of magnitude of the variation we will seek to explain are extremely large. If China really had the same ratio of languages to people as Papua New Guinea, it would have over 200,000 languages.[5] Whilst people might argue about whether Mandarin Chinese is really one language, four, or eight, no one has ever argued that it is 500 or 5,000, still less 100,000 or more. Fourthly, the existence of blurred boundaries and transitional varieties between languages does not undermine the identification of the languages themselves. It merely means that we cannot place the boundaries precisely in those cases.

In view of these justifications, I shall proceed to use counts of languages from standard sources without further discussion, though openly acknowledging their

---

[5] The population of China, multiplied by the ratio of languages to people in Papua New Guinea: 1,178,400,000 × (862 : 3,772,000) = 269,295.

approximate nature. We now return to the problem of explaining the global distribution of languages, with a discussion of how, in general terms, languages are spread across populations.

4.3. Vectors of Language Spread

In this section I briefly consider the nature of the mechanisms by which linguistic norms are spread over populations of people.

As we have seen, the vast majority of the world's languages are confined to the tropics. Most of them are spoken by fairly small numbers of people who live in rural or semi-rural areas. Most have no official status: of the 6,500 languages in the world, only eighty-four are official languages of some nation state.[6] Most languages are not routinely used in a written form, on television, or on the radio. There are a few that present a very different profile: languages such as Mandarin Chinese and English that are standardized and disseminated by publishing industries and other media, and that are the keys of access to large cities and all the institutions of modern states. However, even these languages have acquired their powerful supports only relatively recently. A few generations ago, their vectors of transmission were much more like those of most Third World languages today.

We may thus draw some conclusions about the 'typical' case of the development of a human language in history and prehistory. These are, first, that it is orally transmitted; secondly, that it passes through primary social bonds; thirdly, that state policies are not usually relevant, and, fourthly, that it is encapsulated in the wider system of economic life. I will now explain each of these generalizations in turn.

First, language transmission is basically oral and informal. This means that linguistic norms pass between people who interact face to face. It follows that people with the same speech norms must be connected by social or economic ties, and that lack of face to face interaction between groups will tend to mean that their languages diverge.

Secondly, however, the mere presence of interaction between people is no guarantee of their linguistic homogeneity. In Chapter 2 I described the evidence that sociolinguistic differences can persist despite routine interaction between the people involved. Trade between groups can take place via lingua francas, or pidgins, or bilingual individuals, whilst the underlying differences between their first languages are undiminished.

We also saw in Chapter 2 that what determines whether groups will converge or remain uniform linguistically is a matter of *social identification*. Where indi-

---

[6] This calculation was done using information dating from before the break-up of the USSR. The figure will now be a little higher.

viduals are closely involved enough to want to be identified with each other, they will mutually accommodate their speech behaviour. (This process can also be one-sided, where one party holds greater power or prestige, or has less incentive to get along.) However, they may also trade whilst still actively maintaining ethnolinguistic distance, and we want to know what determines which of these two outcomes results.

The answer seems to lie in the strength and nature of the social bonds involved, and I would like to distinguish between *primary* and *secondary* social bonds. Primary social bonds are relatively enduring, are often formed early in life, and are multivalent. This means that they are not formed for any one specific purpose. Rather they are generalized social linkages that may bring the actors together in many different contexts and at different times. Social bonds within ethno-linguistic groups in non-industrial societies typically appear to have this character; they form a dense web of relationships, which are often reinforced by biological and cultural kinship, and which may form the basis for common ritual activities and celebrations, common defence, common farm work or hunt-ing, gifts, and food sharing, as well as trade narrowly defined. In most societies these primary bonds have also been those on which people have depended for their basic livelihood. Secondary social bonds, by contrast, are based on specific functions, such as a trade in a specialized good like salt or metal, or a specialized service. Purely commercial trade creates only a secondary bond, as reciprocation is immediate, both parties haggle for the best price, and no future moral respon-sibility for the other party is entailed. Secondary bonds are associated with greater social distance than primary ones and are more typical of the relationships between ethnolinguistic groups than those within them. I would argue that they are not themselves sufficient for sociolinguistic identification.

Like almost all dichotomies, the distinction between primary and secondary social bonds simplifies an underlying continuum. Pairings of farming and hunting or herding peoples give a good example of this. The pygmies of central Africa, for example, are specialized hunters, who none the less consume a great deal of their diet in cereals grown by neighbouring farmers. It is unlikely that they could survive reliably by hunting and gathering alone (Bailey *et al.* 1989), and so this relationship is of vital importance to them, although it is in origin a single-purpose rather a multivalent one. Each pygmy group is paired with a particular group of farmers. The interdependence is so great that, in each case, the pygmies have accommodated to the farmers and no longer have a distinctive language (Bailey *et al.* 1992).

Further south, in the Kalahari, San hunter-gatherers also depend upon exchange with neighbouring farmers, yet have remained linguistically distinct (Headland and Reid 1989). In the West African savannah, one finds widespread symbiosis between Fulani pastoralists and cereal farmers, particularly the Hausa. Even the most purely pastoral Fulani consume a high proportion of their calories as cereals that they have traded for milk and other products (Swift 1986: 180). However, the distinction between Hausa and Fulani remains, and a relatively small proportion of those Fulani who are still herders have adopted Hausa as a mother tongue (though most speak it as a lingua franca). The difference in outcome may reflect a difference in the extent of investment in the particular exchange relationship in the different cases. Fulani pastoral networks are extremely extensive, and go well beyond Hausaland, and the San seem to have both a wide choice of trading partners and great flexibility in their own subsistence arrangements. Neither San nor Fulani households are, then, as irreversibly attached to their particular agriculturalist partners as the pygmies, and so they have retained their distinct mother tongues.

Accepting that the distinction is somewhat simplistic, then, we can none the less assert that, in general, people come to have the same first language as those to whom they are linked by primary bonds in the sense I have described.

The third generalization about language transmission is that, for the vast majority of cases, the influence of specialized political and governmental structures is of limited importance. The official languages of modern nation states obviously depart from this pattern, as do all languages in industrialized countries where literacy is high and formal educational institutions extremely influential. Such cases are rare and recent developments, though. As mentioned above, over 98 per cent of languages even today are unofficial, minority tongues, and most persist despite the incorporation of their speakers in wider state, religious, and regional systems. Even in densely populated, early industrialized Europe, 'the virtual identity of language, state and nation was approximated only in the nineteenth century' (Coulmas 1992: 33); and in many European countries minority languages are still spoken. This is despite the fact that the importance of state mechanisms, and their associated media and school systems, have grown enormously in power over the eighteenth and nineteenth centuries. Prior to that in Europe, and in many tropical countries to this day, the state was of restricted importance to the rhythms of most people's lives, and was in general extremely unsuccessful when it attempted to impose one or other mother tongue on its populace. There are, it must be admitted, a few pre-industrial cases where a language spread was associated with a particular political formation. One such example is the spread of vernacular Latin through Europe as part of Roman expansion, but even this case is equivocal; the Romance languages today cover only about 25 per cent of the former Roman Empire, and are restricted to those parts where Latin demographic influence was greatest (Bellwood 1997: 124). There are many more cases where great empires have controlled areas for long periods of time without ordinary country people coming to speak the language of the élite at all, or learning it only as a secondary tongue for use in dealing with government. Thus we must concur with Dyen (1990: 219) that 'the heavy contribution by the language of the conquerors to that of the conquered is an exception rather than the rule'. Overall, it is reasonable to conclude that the determinants of which first language one learns are usually based in very quotidian and local social situations, rather than in courts or parliaments.

The final generalization about language transmission is one that I shall elaborate and explain further in the succeeding sections, but it is as well to sow the idea here. It is that the spread of a language is rooted in an economic system. It might appear that one's choice of primary social associates is a purely social or cultural matter. However, in pre-industrial societies, where relatively little of the circulation of food and labour passes through the wages and money, there is no real distinction between economy and society. An individual's social associates also tend to be those with whom he labours in the fields, or from whom he borrows land, livestock, or seeds, or with whom he combines to appropriate land or construct irrigation systems. Bonds that are social in character are cemented by gifts, and these gifts can involve a very significant proportion of one's staple food, as we shall see for the case of Hausaland below. Above all, it is to social associates that people turn in time of shortage. It seems, in general, that languages are rooted in networks of social bonds that have a real economic importance. Social selection, or the choice of which linguistic norm to identify one's speech with, is, therefore, an economic strategy. Choosing a particular dialect gives access to particular networks of cooperation and exchange that have material as well as social costs and benefits.

We have now discussed in general terms the vectors by which languages are spread. Thus we can return to our basic task of explaining global trends such as those shown on Figure 4.1. It is clear from the foregoing discussion that the formation of any particular ethnolinguistic group will be a complex interplay of many locally specific factors; formation of social bonds will depend upon precise topographical, military, epidemiological, demographic, and cultural situations, as well as more nebulous contingencies such as the rise and fall of local prestige and influence. How, then, can we aim for any kind of general explanation?

It is clear that no one theory will account for the detailed dynamics of every individual language, and many anthropologists would, therefore, hesitate to advance any kind of universal framework. However, there are, as we have seen, very strong regional trends for which I believe general explanations are appropriate. Furthermore, these patterns—the latitudinal trend, the parallel with species diversity—relate to biological or ecological phenomena. This suggests that the appropriate theory will be one that links human agents to their ecological setting. Ecological determinism is viewed with suspicion by many historians and anthropologists. However, I would justify both the elaboration of universal theories and the central place accorded to ecology in the following way.

Until about 200 years ago, the whole of humanity existed under conditions where between 80 and 90 per cent of the people lived directly and more or less completely from the land (Braudel 1985: 49). Most people in the tropics still live in this way. Since prevailing ecological conditions are a major constraint on what the land produces, ecology has had a massive and direct effect on human populations. People have responded to the conditions in which they found themselves with numerous unique cultural responses; myriad ways of organizing production, reproduction, and socio-economic life. However, since life expectancy has always been unremittingly low and infant mortality high, the incentive for finding and adopting ways of life that are well adapted to local conditions has been great. Cultural forms evolve by innovation, experimentation, imitation, and selective retention, and there has been a strong *selection pressure* for those which represent appropriate adaptations.

Just as I have argued that society is basically inseparable from economy, so I would argue that rural economy is inseparable from ecology. It is part of the interaction between human beings and their environment (which includes climate, other species, and other people). In the following section I will try to illustrate this contention by using three specific examples. I will then use the material in these examples to derive the hypothesis that ecological risk is the most important influence on human social networks.

4.4. Case Studies

The three case studies I will now present are intended as illustrations of the interlinkage between society, economy, and ecology, and the implications of this interlinked system for language diversity. The presentation is brief and schematic; the reader is referred to the sources given for other details that are not relevant to our present purposes.

4.4.1. Equatorial horticulturalists: Interior New Guinea

I begin with New Guinea, as it has already come up in our discussion, and because it has many more languages than most continents—some 1,100 when the total for Papua New Guinea is added to that for the Indonesian province of Irian Jaya that forms the western half of the island.

New Guinea is dominated by vast ridges of mountains, but, as we have seen, we cannot assume that the language diversity is a consequence of physical isolation imposed by the topography. In fact, languages and inter-group alliances very often cross over mountain ridges rather than being confined to a single valley (Rappaport 1968: 100). There is also evidence of pre-European trade networks that brought the resources of the coastal areas right up into the highlands (Hays 1993) and vice versa. Widespread borrowing between Papuan languages (Ross 1996) and evidence of inter-group diffusion in material culture (Roberts *et al.*

1995) confirm the picture of boundaries that were generally made and maintained at least partly by people, not by nature alone.

There is very considerable cultural and economic diversity between New Guinea societies. Differences between lowland societies with low population density who rely heavily on fishing and gathering, and the much larger highlands groups who practise intensive tuber farming at altitudes above about 4,000 feet, are especially marked. However, I am for present purposes concerned more with commonalities than differences. In what follows I shall draw particularly on material from groups on the fringes of the highlands, alluding to variations only where it seems necessary for the argument.

Descriptions of New Guinea societies identify a basic unit of social organization as the *local group*. The local group numbers from fifty to several hundred people, and occupies and defends a common territory. Whilst wild resources within the territory are communally owned, gardens cultivated within it are the private property of the family that planted them. The local group can be a clan or a cluster of clans (clans are based on kinship and restrictions on marriage).

Language groups are generally very small. The median number of speakers for a language in Papua New Guinea is 1,000, with a mean number of 3,752.[7] In many cases, the language group is just a single local group occupying a territory of just a few square miles. Elsewhere, there are several local groups in the language group. Such is the case of the Tsembaga Maring described by Rappaport (1968, 1971). The Tsembaga is a local group of around 200 people, and the Maring language group consists of more than twenty such units, giving a total of around 7,000 Maring speakers (Rappaport 1968: 12). The language groups of the biggest highland societies number in the tens of thousands, or, in just a couple of cases, more than 100,000.

The Tsembaga Maring subsist primarily by planting gardens in which sweet potatoes and taro are the main staples. They also cultivate yams, cassava, bananas, manioc, beans, peas, and numerous other crops. Tsembaga informants can name at least 264 edible plants representing thirty-six species (Rappaport 1971: 120). Gardens are cut and burnt from secondary forest, and used once, a new patch of land being cleared for a new garden the next year.

The climate is warm and day length is constant throughout the year, as New Guinea lies within a few degrees of the equator. Rainfall in New Guinea is high. The Maring recognize a wetter and a drier season, though the distinction is not obviously reflected in rainfall statistics, and in fact rainfall throughout New Guinea is quite sufficient for cultivation in every month of the year (Rappaport 1968: app. I). Work clearing gardens generally starts between April and June, with planting taking place after burning of the vegetation in June to September.

---

[7] These statistics are calculated using the database from which the *Ethnologue* 12th edition was compiled. Speaker statistics are available for 817 languages.

Gardens could in fact be started at any other time of the year, and a small secondary garden is often begun between November and April.

A garden begins to yield the main staples twenty or thirty weeks after planting. Rather than being harvested all at once, produce is removed a little at a time, according to need, on an almost daily basis (Rappaport 1971: 127). A garden will continue to produce constantly for between fourteen and twenty-eight months, by which time the next year's garden is already productive. After one usage, a Tsembaga garden is left to lie fallow for fifteen to twenty-five years, though other groups use their gardens two or three times.

The Tsembaga Maring also keep pigs, which are fed on sweet potatoes. From a calorific point of view, this is wasteful, as it would be more energetically efficient for people to consume the tubers directly. However, pigs convert low-protein vegetable matter into high-protein meat. They also have a central function in Maring inter-group ritual and exchange systems, as we shall see.

The subsistence system varies throughout New Guinea. Pig-keeping is less typical of lowland groups, who also use different crops, particularly bananas, and depend more on fishing and gathering forest products, especially sago. The groups who live furthest up in the mountains, such as the Enga and Chimbu, depend very heavily on the sweet potato, which thrives at altitude (Brown 1978: 51–3). However, the year-round pattern of food production seems to be typical of the whole island.

Horticulture provides 99 per cent of the everyday Tsembaga Maring diet (Rappaport 1971: 118) and similar proportions for other highland groups (Morren 1977; Brown 1978). As gardens provide such a reliable and consistent yield through the year, the local group can be entirely self-sufficient in horticultural produce. Although they number only 200, the Tsembaga neither import nor export foodstuffs (Rappaport 1971: 130), with the exception of some pigs. For the Myanmin, a highland fringe group, Morren (1977: 279) reports that less than 3 per cent of calories come from food sources outside the hamlet he studied, which was only a sub-part of the local group. Dwyer and Minnegal (1992) have shown that it would be quite possible for a single *household* amongst the lowland Kubo to be economically self-sufficient. In fact, Kubo households within the local group share produce, but Dwyer and Minnegal argue that this stems from a need to strengthen intra-group relationships, which could be crucial for territorial defence, rather than a horticultural limitation.

Given the enormous potential for self-sufficiency afforded by New Guinea food-production systems, it is not at all surprising that language groups are so small. If a local group needs neither to import nor to export its basic produce, it would seem to have little need for wider communication networks. There are indeed many cases of language groups that consist of no more than one local group. Elsewhere, however, linguistic norms get spread over slightly wider aggregates of people.

There are several mechanisms by which this may occur. Local groups are too small to provide a reliable source of spouses, especially when restrictions on intra-clan marriage are taken into account. Whilst the Tsembaga prefer to marry locally, they often marry with neighbouring Maring groups, though of course mate exchange does not guarantee linguistic uniformity. Maring groups are often at emnity with each other. However, they also unite in various combinations for common defence purposes, and there is a certain fluidity in their boundaries, as local groups may fuse, split, or take in refugees from warfare (Rappaport 1968: 171). The groups, though autonomous, are thus integrated into wider systems of alliances. The most obvious mechanism by which these alliances are maintained are the periodic pig festivals found in many highland societies and known to the Maring as *kaiko* (Rappaport 1968: ch. 5).

Such festivals involve the aggregation of individuals from many different local groups speaking the same language. Trade and gift-giving goes on between individuals of different local groups, and individuals of marriageable age may find spouses. Most conspicuously, a large number of pigs are killed and the meat distributed amongst the groups present. At the *kaiko* witnessed by Rappaport in 1963, over 1,000 individuals participated. They represented seventeen different local groups, and the meat from the slaughter of ninety-six pigs is estimated to have reached 3,000 people. Thus the pig festival serves to strengthen the connections between the scattered and largely autonomous local groups, connections that they may well need for common defence or other concerted action.

Large-scale ritual exchange systems of this kind are untypical of the highland fringe and lowland areas, where language groups are small. On the other hand, in the highest lands, where systems of ceremonial inter-local exchange are most developed and have the widest scale, the language groups are the largest in New Guinea (Brown 1978: 229–33; an example is the Enga *te* cycle: Meggitt 1973). Thus it seems reasonable to assume that such exchange systems are the social channels that keep the linguistic norms of different local groups in touch.

The emphasis in the foregoing paragraphs on the self-sufficiency of local groups, except where ritual exchange systems bound them together, appears to sit oddly with my earlier allusion to the lack of isolation of language groups and the existence of regional trade networks. There is no doubt that such trade networks existed. Here, however, the distinction between primary and secondary social linkages is useful. The regional, inter-group trade networks dealt in plumes, shells, fur, and many other kinds of adornment, tobacco, pottery, stone tools, and salt (Hays 1993). These products are, in general, not necessary to survival. According to Rappaport (1968: 106 ff.), the only regionally traded products that could be said to be of vital importance were salt and stone axes, and the demand for both of these was fairly limited. One needs only a certain quantity of salt, and one stone axe can last a long time. We can, therefore, generalize that the connections between language groups were secondary, in that they provided specific, occasional, usually non-essential goods. The linkages maintained within local groups, and within language groups by common ritual and the web of kinship, were primary in the sense that, even if New Guineans did not often need each other's help to provide food, they relied on each other in times of conflict.

We can summarize in the following way. In New Guinea language groups are very small because people's primary social networks are very small and localized. Secondary networks exist but are not an important enough part of people's lives to cause linguistic convergence. Groupings larger than the household are formed and maintained by ritual and exchange and seem to be motivated at least partly by the need for defensive alliances. Basically, however, the small extent of primary social networks is a product of the ecology of New Guinea: continuous rainfall makes for continuous food production through the year, which in turn allows great self-sufficiency.[8] The other two case studies, from West Africa, show how a different ecological regime leads to quite different social outcomes.

4.4.2. Savannah grain farmers: Hausaland

The Hausa are grain farmers living in the West African savannah, principally in the north of Nigeria and the south of the republic of Niger. To their north are the arid savannahs leading to the Sahara desert, whilst to their south are areas of higher rainfall that are home to numerous groups of yam and cereal farmers.

The Hausa are numerically perhaps the largest linguistic group in tropical Africa (Hill 1982: 25). Estimates of their number vary from 10 million to about 30 million, with much of the difference probably accounted for by the fact that there are many non-Hausa communities who use Hausa as a lingua franca.

The Hausa have an urban tradition stretching back hundreds of years, and the emirates of Hausaland have long exerted a strong political influence on the whole of West Africa (Adamu 1978), as they do in Nigeria today. One might simply argue that the wide extent of the language is due to this influence. After all, at the height of the Sokoto caliphate in the nineteenth century, a large portion of Nigeria and Niger was under the control of a Hausa-speaking empire. I would contend that the spread of the language is not primarily caused by such considerations of 'élite dominance'. The Hausa-dominated political sphere has, for several hundred years, included many non-Hausa-speaking minorities, and,

---

[8] It is a simplification to imply that there are no important ecological fluctuations in the lives of New Guineans. Those at very high altitudes are very dependent on the sweet potato, and are at risk from frost, which can damage the crop severely (Waddell 1975). Frost damage is greatest at highest altitudes. The Enga, whose territory is amongst the highest in New Guinea, are also the largest language group in the interior, with over 160,000 speakers. Enga local groups at the higher ends of the range cultivate alliances with friends and kinsmen lower down. In the event of a period of severe frost, they will migrate down into the territories of their allies. Thus the relatively large social network may have evolved in part as a response to the greater risk, due both to monocrop dependence and frost, that the Enga face as compared to New Guineans at lower altitudes. However, we should also note that population densities in the Highlands are much greater than elsewhere, and this may also be a factor.

although they have generally adopted Hausa as a second language, they have also kept their mother tongues. 'In none of the areas surrounding Hausaland has the process of "Hausanisation" (Hausa acculturation) obliterated completely any of the ethnic groups', writes Adamu (1976: 4). Furthermore, the basic range of the Hausa language may pre-date state formation, as Adamu (1984: 266) claims that there is no other known language indigenous to the area (however, see Last 1985 for an entirely different view).

The great bulk of the Hausa population is rural, 'in the double sense that it lives dispersedly on the farmland or in small villages and depends almost entirely on cultivation and associated rural activities for its livelihood' (Hill 1982: 25). In this sense, the livelihood of most Hausa people is comparable with that of the very small ethnic groups immediately to the south, or for that matter to that of most New Guineans; the difference is that the Hausa language is relatively uniform over a very wide area. I will endeavour to show that, just as in the case of New Guinea, this linguistic outcome is a result of a socio-economic system that in turn is a response to particular ecological conditions.

Hausaland receives around 900mm of annual rainfall (more in the south and less in the north). At around 12° north of the equator, seasonal variation in temperature and day length is not marked. Rainfall, however, is seasonal, being concentrated into a single period of 4–6 months, beginning around April and ending around September (Simmons 1981: 73; Watts 1983). The spatial variation in rainfall is considerable, not just along the north–south axis but more generally, and so the timing and quantity of harvests can differ across the region. During the dry months, cultivation is impossible owing to the lack of water, except on patches of low-lying land with permanent groundwater known as *fadama*.

Staple foods in Hausaland are cereals whose growing patterns correspond well to the availability of water. Planting takes place with the first sustained rains. Millet is harvested three or four months later, whilst the most important crop, sorghum or guinea corn, is harvested in November.

Sorghum is dried and stored in household granaries for use during the six months that will elapse before the next year's early millet is ready. There is always a possibility that these reserves will spoil or prove insufficient. Additional danger lies in the fickleness of the rains, which may arrive late, be deficient, or cause false starts where fields are planted after an initial period of rain, after which there are several dry weeks during which seedlings die. Droughts and crop shortages are recurrent features of the Hausa ecosystem, and so the Hausa have developed mechanisms to provision themselves in the seasons of shortage and in the bad years (Watts 1983).

First, networks of Hausa households (*gidàajee*, which consist of a man, his wives, and children, and sometimes other kin, often nucleated in fairly large villages) are highly interdependent in the provision of food, both cooked and raw (Nicolas 1967; Raynault 1977). Food exchange partly takes the form of gift-giving. In her study of one Hausa village, Simmons (1981) found that the average household gave away 160 lbs of grain in a year, some 22 per cent of the total harvested. These gifts form strong ties between households at some distance from each other. As Watts (1983: 123) puts it, 'Hausa communities . . . were characterized by a rapid circulation of wealth through complex patterns of exchange and gift-giving. . . . The system of gift and counter-gift provided the very fabric of village, and indeed inter-village cohesion.' As well as gifts, foods circulate through trade. All foodstuffs enter informal markets that are also channels of social communication and so act as 'an integrating force in rural Hausaland' (Scott 1976: 215).

During the dry season, Hausa farmers also diversify their activities to generate income. As a rule, every able-bodied Hausa man or woman has an occupation beyond farming that may pursued in the dry season or all year around (Hill 1982: 143–4). In a study of a village in Niger, Curry (1988) found at least twenty-six such occupations, including tanning, weaving, smithing, and above all commerce. Hausa men and women 'have trading in their blood' (Hill 1982: 232–3), and trading journeys during the dry season can take them far afield.

Hausa men also go on seasonal migrations (the *cin rani*) to find work. In general, they flow from north to south, to regions where the rains are earlier or longer and there is agricultural work to be done, or to cities or *fadama* land (Rempel 1981).

In short, a wide variety of mechanisms, including gifts, trade, services, and seasonal migration, serve to create links between distant Hausa households. These links create social cohesion and mutual obligation, and can be turned to as sources of food in the event of localized shortages (Watts 1983). The wide extent of the language must surely have its origin in the wide extent of these links, which are in turn a response to the dangerous highs and lows of the agricultural calendar. For a more extreme example of how seasonality necessitates a wide social network, we now turn to the Hausa's northerly neighbours, the pastoral Fulani and Tuareg.

4.4.3. Nomadic pastoralism: The Fulani and the Tuareg

As one moves north from Hausaland, the rainy season becomes shorter and shorter, and less and less reliable, until, in the Sahara desert, it does not come at all. The vast transitional zone between farmland and desert, which stretches right across West Africa, is known loosely as the *sahel*, from an Arabic word for shore. It is inhabited by groups of nomadic pastoralists, the largest of which are the Fulani (who speak Fulfulde) and the Tuareg (who speak Tamashek). The economic systems of these groups are centred in the sahel but also exploit both the desert areas to the north (particularly in the Tuareg case) and the agricultural savannahs to the south.

In terms of numbers of speakers, Fulfulde and Tamashek are smaller languages than Hausa. This is because the population density of the areas in which they are spoken is very low. In terms of the land area over which they are current, however, they are much bigger than Hausa. Indeed, by this criterion, Fulfulde is one of the most widespread languages in the world. As in the two previous case studies, I will endeavour to show that the wide extent of the languages is a result of the socio-economic system of the people, which in turn is influenced by the ecological regime in which they live.

Sahelian pastoralists rely on animals and animal products almost exclusively for income. However, their diets contain very significant proportions of grain in almost all cases (Swift 1986; Legge 1989: 81). Grain is obtained by direct exchange with non-pastoral groups in return for animal products. The basic investment of the pastoralist economy is thus in herds of animals; as one Fulani pastoralist observed, 'The cow is our insurance, our certitude, and it can be milked morning and night, and it will always be with us, our certitude is to have a good, growing, healthy flock of animals' (quoted in Legge 1989: 84).

The most fundamental danger of pastoral life is the loss of livestock through lack of pasture, lack of water, or disease. The 'loss of a substantial proportion of the family herd means immediate destitution. This is a risk that every herdsman faces several times in his life, and is a major determinant of his behaviour' (Swift 1973: 73).

Sahelian pastoralists do indeed exploit a precarious niche. The areas to the south have more abundant rainfall and hence a better supply of grazing. However, those areas are densely populated with farmers, which means competition for land and water. The northern zone is largely empty of people, and so in the brief rainy season when pasture is growing it represents a remarkable unexploited resource. However, for most of the year it is too dry for grass to grow. The nomadic pastoral system represents a solution to this ecological dilemma. During the rainy season, both Fulani and Tuareg herds are moved north, as far as the limits of rainfall will allow, to exploit empty seasonal pastures. As these dry up, around September or October, the herds come south. They spend the dry season moving around the southern part of their ranges, where they overlap with farming communities. The herds are let onto farmland after the harvest to eat the crop residues and manure the land (an exchange that is beneficial to both parties). Competition for space with farming communities is not intense at this time, since no crops are growing, except on waterlogged *fadama* land, which is prized by both farmers and herders. The most critical period is at the end of the dry season, when crop residues are all finished and the land is at its driest. As soon as the rains begin in earnest, farming communities start to plant crops and the herds flow northwards, back to their rainy-season pastures.

Sahelian pastoralists thus use almost constant mobility to exploit their fluctuating environment, with individual households covering hundreds of kilometres during the year. These migratory orbits also change from year to year, according to particular conditions. However, even this is not sufficient guarantee of safety. A herd of animals can survive only a very few days without food and water, and there is always a danger of not finding free pasture in time. Changing conditions can be mitigated by selling stock, or changing the ratios of camels, cows, sheep, and goats, which have slightly different diets. Under extreme conditions, individuals may leave pastoralism altogether, for agriculture or labouring.

Pastoralists also, crucially, depend on socio-economic relationships with other households. Local groups are somewhat fluid, with different households coming together and drifting apart as the needs of the animals dictate. Social networks, however, are extensive, and animals are borrowed and exchanged through them. In the case of the Niger Fulani, animal loans fall into several categories (Legge 1989: 84). Loans of *dialle* animals are a form of short-term emergency aid. The recipient has the use of the animal's milk as a food source, but must return it, along with any offspring it has borne. When a man is starting a herd, or rebuilding one after a loss, he may borrow *habbanae* animals to do so. These are kept until they have borne three offspring, the calves being kept by the borrower to build up his herd. The *habbanae* system does more than just provide a favour to the borrower, a favour that would presumably be reciprocated in time of reversed fortunes. Even wealthy herders may be both lender and borrower of *habbanae* animals at all times. This is because having some animals in another herd not only cements a social bond with that herder, but is a useful fallback if one's own herd is hit by drought or disease.

The exchange of livestock is just one of the mechanisms by which extensive contact is maintained between scattered camps of pastoralists throughout the region. Vast networks of social linkages, covering more than a million square kilometres, give desert-margin groups access to refuges and relief in time of need (Colson 1979: 23–4; Fuchs 1983, 1984). The Niger Fulani are thought to be able to maintain their herds through periods of drought 'in part because of their wide networks of kinsmen throughout West Africa' (Berg 1976: 24). If Fulani households have networks of kin they can turn to scattered throughout West Africa, it is unsurprising that their language should be found in substantially inter-intelligible form throughout West Africa, as indeed it is (Mann and Dalby 1980: 32).

Thus the ecological conditions of the *sahel* favour wide orbits of movement and exchange, which in turn produce extensive social networks. These wide networks produce languages vastly more widespread than those of wet tropical areas such as New Guinea. In the next section I will try to build these observations about the relationship between ecology, social network, and language into a predictive theory that can be tested.

4.5. Ecological Risk as a Universal Constraint

The three case studies have shown how different ecological regimes favour different kinds of social networks, which in turn produce different-sized linguistic groups. In this section I will derive a general hypothesis about the relationship between ecology, social network, and language diversity that will then be tested in the following section.

Individuals in any non-industrial society have to simultaneously solve many different ecological problems. These range from coping with disease, to providing fuel, fertilizer, and drinking water, to optimizing inter-group relations and population pressure. Whilst recognizing the diversity of these factors, a case can be made that one variable can be identified which has a pre-eminent influence on many aspects of life, especially the formation of linguistic groups. I will suggest that that factor may be described as *ecological risk*.

The real difference between the New Guinea case and the West African ones is in the amount of climatic variation that has to be faced. In New Guinea, not only is rainfall constant through the year, but consistently high from year to year. There are thus no large fluctuations in food supply from one month to the next or from one year to the next. In both the Hausa and the Fulani/Tuareg cases, variations from season to season cause people to depend on distant food suppliers at certain times of year, and the possibility of bad years necessitates the formation of a large number of social bonds that can be turned to for food provisioning when the need arises.

These two variables, seasonal variation and inter-year variation, can be subsumed into the single category of ecological risk. Ecological risk can be loosely defined as the probability of a household facing a temporary shortfall, at whatever timescale, in food production. In recent years, evidence has been accumulating that risk and variability have profound effects on the dynamics of non-industrial societies. The importance of periodic famine in the non-industrial world is widely recognized (Braudel 1985: 73 ff.). In most societies, seasonal fluctuations in climate are related to seasonal fluctuations in births, deaths, and nutritional status (Chambers *et al.* 1981; Bailey *et al.* 1992).[9]

These patterns of fluctuation can remain remarkably consistent in particular regions for long periods of time, which leads Shaw (1996: 113) to suggest that they provide a historical 'fingerprint' identification of populations' demographic

---

[9] Interestingly, it has been claimed that seasonal fluctuations in births increase with distance from the equator, and may be reduced or absent in equatorial climates (Brewis *et al.* 1996). Thus birth seasonality patterns are broadly correlated with the same external factors as linguistic diversity (Bailey *et al.* 1992). Lam and Miron (1991), however, suggest that the pattern of birth seasonality is not so simple, and indeed Condon and Scaglion (1982) show that, whilst there are cases of climate-related birth fluctuations, there are also cases where seasonality of births follow from cultural calenders that are unrelated to climate.

regime. I would go further and suggest that they provide clues about the basic ecological constraints under which social systems are evolving.

Theoretical attention in anthropology has been concentrated on the mechanisms that evolve in different populations to cope with risk (e.g. Cashdan 1985, 1990; Minnis 1985; Huss-Ashmore *et al.* 1988; DeGarine and Harrison 1988; Halstead and O'Shea 1989). Four key strategies may be identified (Halstead and O'Shea 1989: 3; Colson (1979: 21) divides them into five rather than four but her schema is basically the same). These are diversification, storage, mobility, and exchange.

Farmers diversify their agricultural activities by employing several crops that mature at different times or have different resistances to disease. They may also cultivate scattered plots of land, to spread their investments (Winterhalder 1990). Pastoralists have a balance of different types of animal in their herds for much the same reason. At times of scarcity people diversify their diets to include more wild products or products that would not be valued at other times. Finally, when agriculture is not productive, people diversify into other income-generating occupations, as we saw very clearly in the Hausa case.

Storage is an important strategy, though limited by various factors. Hausa farmers store food in their granaries, as we have seen, though these are always vulnerable to pest damage, rotting, and theft. Furthermore, food can never be stored indefinitely, and so storage may not be an effective buffer against a succession of bad years. Pastoralists such as the Fulani store their food 'on the hoof' by maintaining herds as large as they can manage (Legge 1989), but increasing herd size causes higher costs in terms of finding adequate food and water for the animals, as well as increased animal mortality and reduced fertility (Swift 1986: 178). Storage, then, is a crucial response to risk, but heavy dependence on it has risks of its own.

The mobility response was clearly illustrated by both the seasonal migration of Hausa farmers and the annual circuits of Fulani and Tuareg. Different types of society have different potentials for mobility: the mobility of farmers is constrained by the need to protect and tend the land they have invested their time in. Pastoralists' investment is primarily in their herds, so their mobility is a function mainly of the mobility of their animals. Hunter-gatherers, on the other hand, have little in the way of accumulated capital, and so their mobility is potentially much greater. I will return to these differences in Section 4.8.

The final strategy, and the key one from the current perspective, is exchange. By forming networks of social bonds over a wide area, people gain access to the resources of different localities and different producers. By giving gifts at time of plenty, people form ties of obligation to which they can look when their own supplies become scarce. The importance of exchange as a buffer was very clear in the West African cases, just as its absence in New Guinea corresponded to the relative absence of risk.

Social exchange is very important with respect to language diversity for the following reason. Exchange creates bonds between the participants. If those bonds become strong and important enough for the actors to identify with each other, they will serve as channels for the spread of linguistic norms. Thus the extent of the linguistic group will be a function of household exchange networks. Where exchange combines with mobility, as in the Fulani case, the potential for widespread languages is especially great, as seasonal migration circuits carry linguistic norms over great distances. Mobility alone cannot spread languages widely, however. It must be accompanied by close links between people at distant locations, or no linguistic accommodation will occur.

Forming social ties has very considerable costs. Allies must be visited, which takes time and energy. Gift-giving and festivals that integrate different villages can seriously deplete production surpluses. Given these costs, and the chance of non-reciprocation by allies, the return on investment of energy in social exchange, in the long run, is less than the input. Social exchange is thus a useful way of reducing variation in the food supply, but one that is likely to also reduce the mean. In view of the cost of social networks, groups of households that can be self-sufficient have a strong incentive to be so, and we saw in Chapters 2 and 3 that, once groups have fissioned into socially cohesive subunits, linguistic differentiation will follow.

Overall, then, we should expect people to form social networks that are as extensive as necessary to ensure reliable food provision under normal circumstances, but not more so, unless there are other strong reasons present, such as the need for common defence against other groups. We can thus predict a general correlation between the degree of ecological risk of the environment people live in and the average size of language groups.

The social response to ecological risk is effective for two slightly different reasons, and these give rise to two different hypotheses to be tested. First, increasing the spatial extent of a social network gives individuals in it access to more micro-environments and types of land, which may have food products available at different times. This *spatial averaging* of ecological risk leads to the prediction that the spatial extent of language groups should increase as the degree of ecological risk they are exposed to increases. Secondly, increasing the number of productive households in a social network decreases the variation experienced by all of them as a simple consequence of the law of large numbers (as long as there is some degree of statistical independence between them). This *numerical averaging* leads to the prediction that the number of individuals in a language group should increase as the degree of ecological risk increases.

In the next two sections I will test the two predictions of the ecological-risk theory against the country-by-country global language data from Grimes (1993). The two predictions would be equivalent only in a world where population density was the same everywhere. I will therefore test them separately.

4.6. Testing the Theory: Methods

In order to test the ecological-risk theory, one needs, first, a measure of language diversity for each country, and, secondly, a measure of the ecological risk associated with the climate of that country. For the first, I use simply the number of languages spoken in the country today. For the second, I use climatic data from each country to calculate a measure called the *growing season*. This has been found by agronomists and ecologists to correlate closely with direct measures of plant growth (Le Houérou 1989) and has already proved useful as a proxy for ecological risk in the context of West Africa (Nettle 1996b).[10]

This measure gives the average number of months per year in which useful plant growth, and hence food, can be produced, for any point at which there is a weather station. A month is included in the growing season if the average daily temperature is more than 6°C and the total precipitation in millimetres is more than twice the average temperature in centigrade. The growing season is an inverse measure of within-year ecological risk: the more growing months there are, the less the risk. Risk obviously exists at other timescales, too. If rainfall were abundant through most years, but there were occasional drought years, then communities would have to adapt to the possibility. In many cases, though, rainfall variability from year to year is correlated with its variability within the year (e.g. Oguntoyinbo 1981, for West Africa), so the measure of within-year risk used here is probably a reasonable proxy for between-year risk, too.

The analysis is restricted to the tropics. The tropics are strictly defined as the area between the tropics of Capricorn and Cancer, but, for the present purposes, the broader definition of the area between 30°N and 30°S is preferable, as it captures more of the area of the climatic regimes we know as 'equatorial' and 'tropical'. The analysis has not been extended to the temperate latitudes for a number of reasons. First, the available measures of ecological risk take account only of rainfall and average temperature, and thus cease to realistically reflect the possibilities of food production as one moves out of the tropical zone. In European countries, for example, plant growth at certain seasons is more affected by night frosts and day length than daytime temperature and rainfall, and is generally much slower than in the tropics. Secondly, the economies of the tropical countries are more rural and more dominated by subsistence activities than those of most of the temperate countries. Thirdly, most temperate countries have far less language diversity than tropical ones, so there is much less variation to work with from a statistical point of view.

---

[10] There are a large number of alternative approaches to the measurement of climatic seasonality (see Walsh 1981). The Growing Season measure adopted here is similar to Walsh's Mean Dry Months. In most tropical areas the various measures correlate well with each other, and also with other climatic variables such as total rainfall (Nettle 1996b: 418–19).

Very small countries are also likely to produce misleading results. Many languages are spoken in the Gambia, for example, but the Gambia is a very narrow strip of land, and every one of the languages is also spoken in Senegal or elsewhere. It would thus be misleading to calculate the diversity of the Gambia as if all of its languages were contained within its small area. For this reason, countries under 50,000 km^2 in area have been excluded, with the exception of Vanuatu and the Solomon Islands, which, despite their small sizes, both have a large number of languages that are not spoken anywhere else.

The mean growing season was found for all remaining countries using meteorological records (Wernstadt 1972). These give data for a number of weather stations that varies from one to over 200 per country, over a time period that varies from a few years to fifty or more. The stations are designed to be distributed evenly around each country. Since countries are not ecological units, and are often large enough to span many ecological regimes, there is in some cases a danger of producing a meaningless 'average' climate that does not correspond to that experienced by any of its communities. As a safeguard against this, countries where the standard deviation of the growing seasons from the different weather stations was greater than two months were excluded. These countries were Algeria, Australia, Bolivia, Brazil, Ecuador, Ethiopia, Guatemala, Honduras, Kenya, Madagascar, Mexico, Nicaragua, Nigeria, Paraguay, Peru, South Africa, Sri Lanka, Sudan, and Venezuela.

The two predictions of the ecological-risk theory can be restated in terms of languages per country as follows. The spatial averaging prediction gives Hypothesis 1:

> *Hypothesis 1.* The greater the ecological risk, the fewer languages there will be in a country of a given size.

The numerical averaging prediction gives Hypothesis 2:

> *Hypothesis 2.* The greater the ecological risk, the fewer languages there will be in a country of a given population.

These hypotheses were tested by regressing the number of languages for each country against the average growing season and either the area of the country (Hypothesis 1) or the population of the country (Hypothesis 2). The area (km^2) and population (thousands; mid-year estimates for 1991) figures come from the *UN Demographic Yearbook 1993*.

Obviously, both the ecological and linguistic variables are highly approximate, the former because of the simplicity of the formula and the unevenness of the data, the latter because of the inherent difficulties involved in counting languages. We should thus expect at best an approximate relationship.

4.7. Testing the Theory: Results

The Appendix gives the number of living languages, population in thousands, area in km², number of complete weather station records, and mean growing season in months for seventy-four countries, including, for the sake of completeness, the countries with variable climates. In order to reduce skewness and kurtosis for the regression analysis, natural logs were taken of the area, languages, and population variables. The equations produced by the regression analyses are all listed in Table 4.1.

TABLE 4.1. *Results of multiple regression analyses of the country-by-country language-diversity data.*

Regression	A	B	C	*r*	*d.f.*	*p*
Langs on Area and MGS	0.53	0.24	−4.77	0.65	52	<0.001
Langs on Area and MGS, South America excluded	0.43	0.30	−3.64	0.81	45	<0.001
Langs on Area and MGS, Asia/Pacific only	0.49	0.32	−4.22	0.87	15	<0.001
Langs on Area and MGS, Africa only	0.40	0.26	−3.06	0.74	27	<0.001
Langs on Population and MGS	0.34	0.18	−0.65	0.64	52	<0.001
Langs on Population and MGS, South America excluded	0.25	0.23	0.10	0.77	45	<0.001
Langs on Population and MGS, Asia/Pacific only	0.24	0.26	0.02	0.82	15	<0.001
Langs on Population and MGS, Africa only	0.23	0.19	0.51	0.67	27	<0.001

Note: The equations have the form ln[Langs] = A ln[Area] + B [Mean Growing Season] + C, or ln[Langs] = A ln[Population] + B [Mean Growing Season] + C. The correlation coefficient is represented by *r*; *d.f.* is the number of degrees of freedom of the regression, *p* is the level of significance of the regression.

Hypothesis 1. The greater the ecological risk, the fewer languages there will be in a country of a given size.

The multiple regression shows that the hypothesized relationship does indeed hold for the world's countries. The equation produced is the first listed in Table 4.1. Figure 4.2 shows the relationship between the number of languages and the mean growing season once the area of the country has been controlled for.

It is immediately apparent from Figure 4.2 that the South American countries

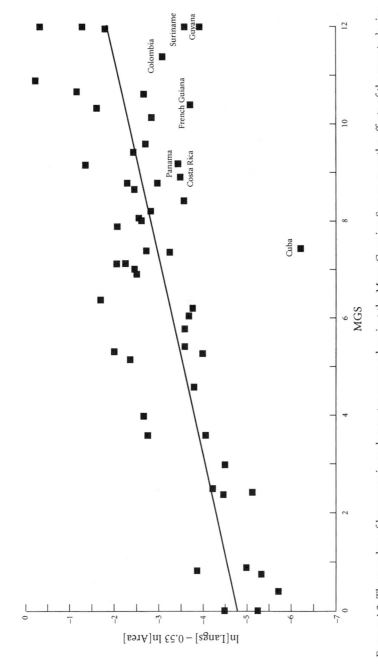

FIGURE 4.2. The number of languages in each country regressed against the Mean Growing Season once the effects of the country's size have been controlled for

Note: The South American countries are labelled.

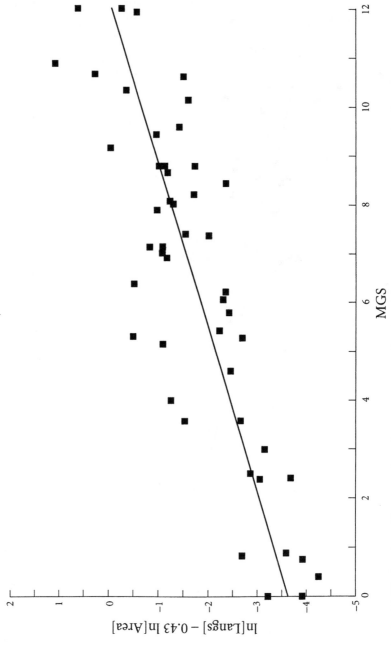

FIGURE 4.3. The number of languages in each country regressed against the Mean Growing Season once the effects of the country's size have been controlled for, with the South American countries excluded

fall well below the rest of the distribution. There are a number of possible reasons for this. One is the fact that only a tiny fraction of tropical South America is populated (less than 5 per cent according to Partridge 1989: 5). It follows that there will be many fewer groups than one would expect on the basis of area. Also, the vast majority of the population is coastal, of recent arrival, and Spanish- or Portuguese-speaking, and many languages have been lost. There are a number of peoples whose demise is known about, but many more who must have disappeared without record, principally through disease (Crosby 1986). In Cuba, the most extreme outlier in Figure 4.3, the indigenous population was decimated within a very few years of European contact (Niddrie 1971: 82). Thus it is no surprise that there are fewer groups than one might expect.

If the South American countries are excluded, the regression relationship is much improved, as Figure 4.3 and the second equation in Table 4.1 show.

The relationship between language diversity and climate is not just a product of comparing different continents. It also holds very clearly within the Asia/Pacific and African groups of countries. The relationships for each of the continents considered separately are shown in Figures 4.4 and 4.5. The regression equation for Africa and that for the Asia/Pacific are remarkably similar to each other (rows 3 and 4 of Table 4.1). This suggests that the relationship is no accident of one continent's geography, and that we are right in claiming that ecological risk is a powerful and universal determinant. Unfortunately, the data from South America are too few (7 data points) to obtain an independent multiple regression; and anyway the South American situation has been terribly disrupted in the last 500 years, as noted above.

Hypothesis 2. The greater the ecological risk, the fewer languages there will be in a country of a given population.

Once again, multiple regression shows that the hypothesized relationship does indeed hold. The relationship is shown in Figure 4.6. As before, the South American countries sit below the rest of the distribution. Excluding them improves the relationship (Figure 4.7). The relationship also holds independently in the two major continents (the last two equations in Table 4.1). The predictions of both hypotheses, then, are clearly met.

If the countries with very variable growing seasons, which were excluded (see Section 4.6) are included, the significance of the relationships is not changed, the r values being slightly lowered (Hypothesis 1: $r = 0.60$, $d.f. = 71$, $p < 0.001$; Hypothesis 2: $r = 0.57$, $d.f. = 71$, $p < 0.001$; South America included in both cases).

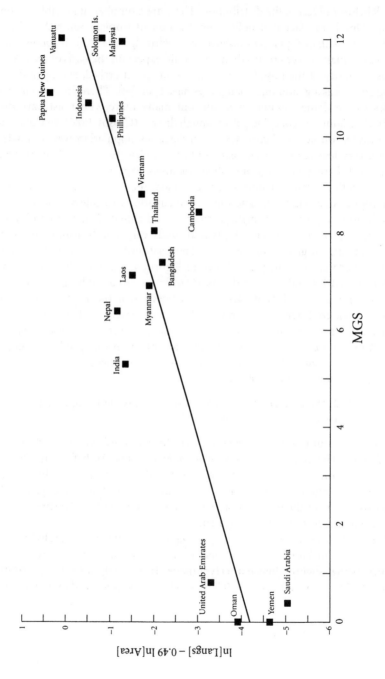

FIGURE 4.4. The number of languages in each country in Asia and the Pacific regressed against the Mean Growing Season once the effects of the country's size have been controlled for

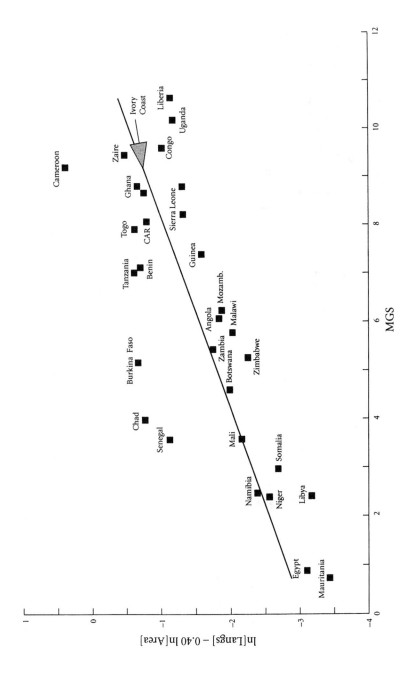

FIGURE 4.5. The number of languages in each country in Africa regressed against the Mean Growing Season once the effects of the country's size have been controlled for

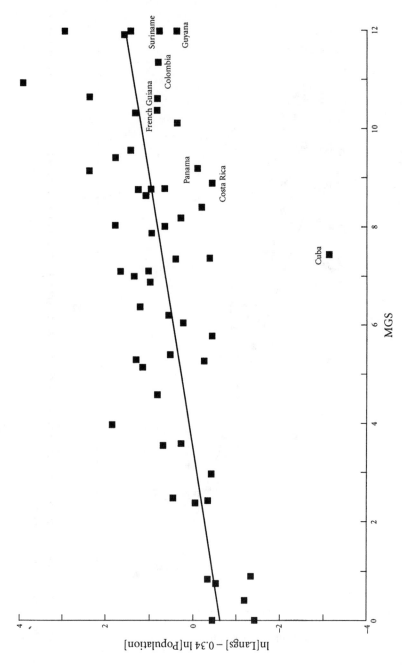

FIGURE 4.6. The number of languages in each country regressed against the Mean Growing Season once the effects of the country's population have been controlled for

Note: The South American countries are labelled.

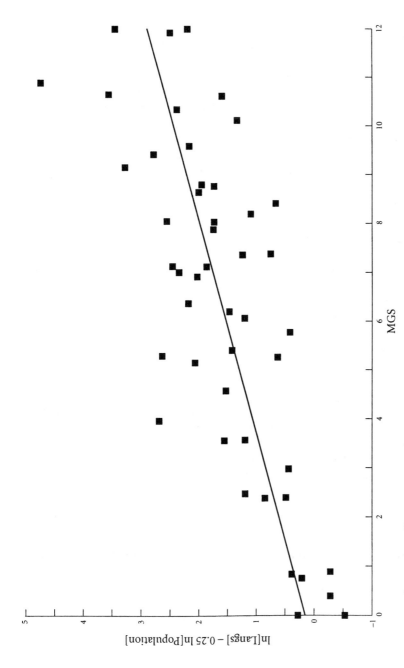

FIGURE 4.7. The number of languages in each country regressed against the Mean Growing Season once the effects of the country's population have been controlled for, with the South American countries excluded

4.8. Hunter-Gatherers

We predicted in Section 4.5 that hunter-gatherer communities would respond in a different way from farmers and herders to ecological risk. Farmers in particular are constrained to stay on their lands except in the most extreme cases of shortfall. Thus, where ecological risk is high, they have to employ systems of exchange that bring resources to them. Hunter-gatherers, on the other hand, are highly mobile, and, faced with scarcity, can simply move in such a way as to track resources. Hunter-gatherers do mitigate risk by sharing and exchange (Wiessner 1977; Kaplan *et al.* 1990; for formal economic models, see Winterhalder 1986), but their groups remain small as risk is primarily dealt with by mobility.

In terms of our hypotheses, then, hunter-gatherer groups should consist of fewer people than those of farmers or pastoralists in similar environments. As risk increases, the numerical size of hunter-gather groups would not be expected to increase as much as those of farmers or pastoralists, though their spatial extent may increase, because the foraging circuits over which they move will become larger, and the number of different groups that can be supported in a given area will decrease.

These predictions seem to be borne out by the evidence. In Africa, the San communities of Botswana number between a few hundred and about 10,000; Tswana farmers at the same latitude number 3 million or more (Grimes 1993). The best test of the prediction comes from comparing Australia, which is the one major country populated entirely by hunter-gatherers in pre-colonial times, with the rest of the distribution.

Australia is one of the countries whose growing season has a standard deviation of greater than two months, and is therefore excluded from many of the analyses. Its growing season value is also rather unrepresentative; the average of 6.0 months reflects the fact that there are many more weather stations around the coast than in the interior, and a more accurate value for the whole land mass would be much lower. None the less, bearing these limitations in mind, we can examine where Australia falls in the total distribution of countries.

There are several estimates available for the pre-colonial population of Australia. We can thus use the regression equation to predict how many languages it should have had if it patterned like an average country. This is done by substituting a population estimate, and the mean-growing-season value of 6.0 months into the best regression equation for ln[Langs] on ln[Population] and Mean Growing Season (the sixth row of Table 4.1).

The classic ethnographic population estimates are around 251,000 (Yengoyan 1968: 190). Using this figure, the number of languages predicted for Australia by the equation is 17.53. Recent historical and archaeological work has suggested a far larger population; perhaps more like 750,000 (White and Mulvaney 1987). This figure gives a prediction of 129.28 languages.[11]

The number of languages listed as living by Grimes (1993) is in fact 234, with at least another thirty-two known to have gone extinct in the last 200 years.[12] This total suggests the number of people per language before 1788 to have been between around 1,000 and 3,000. The 266-language total is much greater than either of the regression predictions derived above. The observed number of languages is between twice (using the high population estimate) and fifteen times (using the low one) the number that the pattern in the rest of the world would predict. Full of uncertainties as it is, this calculation does seem to confirm that hunter-gatherer groups tend to consist of fewer individuals for a given ecological regime than farming or pastoralist ones, thus giving relatively greater language diversity.

It was also predicted that, with increasing risk, the numerical size of hunter-gatherer communities would increase less than that of other communities, though their spatial extent might increase. This also seems to be confirmed by aboriginal Australia. The numerical size of the aboriginal tribe was relatively constant, at around 500 individuals (Yengoyan 1968: 188–9), slightly less on the coast.[13] The spatial extent of the foraging territory it covered varied with rainfall. Ranges were largest in risky arid areas and smallest where rainfall was abundant (Birdsell 1953). Thus hunter-gatherers average out ecological risk primarily by moving, whereas less mobile people have to do it by social exchange, which makes the resources come to them.

The most interesting implication of this difference between hunter-gatherers and farmers or herders is that there would have been more language diversity in the world, certainly in relative terms and perhaps absolutely, before the origin of agriculture. This fact will be important in the next chapter, where we consider how global patterns of language diversity change over time.

---

[11] The 95% confidence intervals for these predictions are very large, because the dependent variable in the equation is a logarithm, and a small change in this translates into a change of an order of magnitude or more when anti-logs are taken to produce a predicted number of languages. The intervals are: for the low-population estimate: 3.48 to 88.15; for the high-population estimate: 16.99 to 944.40. I should note that the observed number of languages falls within the 95% confidence interval for the predicted number using the high-population estimate.

[12] The accuracy of these figures is subject to dramatic change owing to the crisis extinction currently observed in the languages of Australia.

[13] This is probably a simplification, but it is often repeated in the ethnographic literature on Australia. Also note that the tribe in this sense is not coterminous with a language, though it may be a dialectal unit; there can be several tribes to one language.

4.9. Conclusions

The results of this chapter suggest that ecological risk has been an extremely important factor—probably the most important single factor at a global level—in the development of people's strategies of group formation and communication. Several other factors that have not been examined in detail here would also need consideration if more of the considerable variance in the model were to be accounted for. The difficulty of movement—due to relief, thick jungle and so on—and the availability of different means of transport—canoes or horses, for example—could greatly affect the costs and benefits of social exchange. Of course, adequate transport is a necessary, but not a sufficient, condition for forming a large social network; there must also be a positive benefit from doing so, which brings us back to the subsistence demands discussed here.

More consideration might also be required of the relationship between socio-political evolution and language spread. Societies in seasonally dry or seasonally cold environments produce periodic surpluses, as we have seen, and must evolve social mechanisms to spread these out through time and space. However, such surpluses can be extracted as tribute or monopolized by powerful individuals, and this pathway leads to the formation of stratified societies and of states. Once states are in place, they can set up economic, religious, and military institutions that can contribute to linguistic homogenization. As I said in Section 4.3, I believe élite institutions have been the determinants of language spread only in a tiny minority of cases until very recently. This area does, however, need further exploration.

Many other locally specific factors contribute to the evolution of particular language maps: disease, topography, and unrepeatable confluences of local prestige, culture, and demography. However, the strength of the correlations justifies our large-scale approach to the problem, and suggests that no factor has been as strong or general as ecological risk. This means that the relationship between language diversity and species diversity is a general one, since ecological risk factors also influence species diversity (Nichols 1992: 316).

A number of puzzles remain, however. Perhaps the most obvious problem for the theory is the following one: if people form social networks with others within a certain radius around them, and if, furthermore, they acquire their linguistic norms from those social contacts, then why are there bounded groups with different languages rather than continua of dialects? I will clarify the problem with an example. Let us consider an idealized chain of villages, numbered 1 to 9. Let us then assume that each village tends to need economic links with two others to provide its food. One might therefore expect village 2 to exchange with villages 1 and 3, village 3 with villages 2 and 4, village 4 with villages 3 and 5, and so on. On this assumption, we might expect the linguistic norms of village 2 to be halfway between those of 1 and 3; those of village 3 halfway between 2 and 4, and so on. In other words, instead of discrete languages, there would be a chain of smooth variation where the difference between the speech of the villages increased continuously with distance. Now such chains do exist in some areas, and it would be a mistake to exaggerate the sharpness of ethnic or linguistic boundaries, but many of the small tropical societies I have been describing are better characterized in the language of discrete groups than that of continua (indeed, that seems to be how the peoples themselves characterize them). It is as if, in our example, the result were three ethnolinguistic groups (villages 1–3, 4–6, 7–9), with definite boundaries and sharp breaks between the languages, and with the peripheral villages ignoring one neighbour in favour of a more distant ally.

I think the reasons why boundaries become sharp bring us back to the arguments about social selection and social marking from Chapters 2 and 3. Individuals rely on the cooperation and assistance of their friends and allies. One way of getting access to such assistance is to identify oneself as part of a particular group, which is likely to be defined in opposition to some other group, especially given that one of its recurrent functions may be collective defence. Dialect, as we have seen, is a primary vehicle for social identification. Consider the case of an individual who lives on the boundary between two diverging but still mutually intelligible dialects, A and B. This individual could in principle acquire and use an intermediate dialect formed from the 'averaging' of the speech to which he is exposed on either side, and this would be intelligible in both communities. However, what would be the social pay-off for so doing? He would not really be a member of A, since his speech was that of some kind of stranger, and he would not be accorded the rights or status accorded to an insider. On the other hand, he would not enjoy greater social success in B. In fact, his intermediate dialect, rather than being *more* useful for being intelligible in both places, would be valueless in many respects. Thus, such boundary individuals probably have a high incentive to identify strongly one way or the other, thus contributing to the further separation of A and B. Of course, the value of an intermediate dialect would change rapidly were A and B suddenly to need each other—for example, in response to a common external threat. Boundary individuals in that case might suddenly find themselves holders of considerable social capital. By such processes, dialects are born and die.

In this chapter we have assumed that the language diversity of the world is at some kind of equilibrium, determined by the socio-economic organization of communities in different areas, which is in turn affected by the ecological regime in which they live. This is not a static equilibrium, of course, as individual communities ceaselessly form and fission, but a dynamic equilibrium in which the general level of language diversity is approximately constant. Does this mean, however, that the amount of language diversity in the world has been the same since people have inhabited it and will be the same in the future? In the next chapter I will argue that this is not so. The diversity of languages we have examined in this chapter is the equilibrium level of the post-Neolithic, but pre-industrial, world. The equilibrium level of diversity before the Neolithic, and that in the future when the full effects of economic take-off have been felt, are no doubt very different. In the next chapter, then, we consider how the level of language diversity has changed and will change with time.

5 Language Diversity: Changes in Time

5.1. Introduction

The previous chapter examined the distribution of languages in space. The approach was to take a snapshot of languages at one point in time (the present day), and assume that the pattern observed was some sort of equilibrium. The assumption of equilibrium proved to be useful, in so far as the patterns we observed did, by and large, bear a systematic relationship to ecology and geography.

The equilibrium we observed was one that had arisen as farming and herding societies gradually, unconsciously, adapted their social systems to the ecological regime in which they found themselves. Ninety-nine per cent of contemporary human communities (and 99.997 per cent of human beings) depend for their food on agriculture and herding; these have been the dominant modes of human subsistence for at least 6,000 years (Ellen 1994: 201, 214). Even those few hunter-gatherer societies that persist have access to farmed products, and there is some doubt as to whether they could survive without them (Bailey *et al.* 1989). Thus the patterns of human geography we see today are very much the patterns of the Neolithic, the farming, and the herding age. We can infer when those patterns arose because archaeologists can date the origin and spread of the Neolithic in different parts of the world with reasonable confidence.

Such evidence as we can bring to bear suggests that the world's language diversity would have looked different before the rise of farming. Looking to the future, languages are now dying out at an unprecedented rate—Krauss (1992) suggests that 90 per cent will disappear by the end of the twenty-first century—and so we can also predict that it will look very different once the full effects of the industrial age have spread around the world. This chapter examines these changes in language diversity with time. As the theme of the chapter is a one-off historical process rather than a comparison of different geographical areas, the mode of writing will have to be somewhat different. Where the last chapter was organized around hypotheses to be tested and data used to do so, the present one takes the form of a necessarily speculative chronological account with historical or archaeological evidence marshalled where possible.

A useful starting point for our enquiries is the framework proposed by Dixon

(1997). Dixon contends that the history of languages, at a macroscopic level, has consisted of a series of equilibria, during which the number and general size of languages have been constant for long periods, interspersed with a few punctuations, during which many languages have been driven extinct whilst others have been born. The motivation for Dixon's proposal is the search for an alternative to the simplistic picture of language history which often seems to underlie work in historical linguistics. In this picture, evolution at the level of whole languages is principally of the ramifying, treelike variety, and this ramification proceeds at an approximately constant rate (a constant rate is an explicit axiom of glottochronology, and of Nichols's work (1990, 1992)—see Chapter 6 and Nettle (forthcoming *b*)—but it is assumed more tacitly in many other approaches). Dixon is keen to point out that there are periods of rapid ramification, and the results of these periods are the neat trees of divergence of many of the language families with which we are familiar, such as Indo-European and Bantu. However, periods of ramification are not necessarily the norm. Rather, such episodes have specific human causes, such as the colonization of new lands, or the demographic expansions consequent on new technologies, the most notable of which is agriculture (Renfrew 1987, 1991; Bellwood 1997).

Between the rapid expansions, which Dixon refers to as punctuations, are long periods lacking such drastic demographic or social upheaval, which Dixon calls equilibria. He suggests that, during equilibria, much language change may be of the diffusive, convergent type, as societies interact, intermarry, fission, and fuse. After a long period of equilibrium, because of this diffusion, neat family trees for whole languages may become impossible to draw. This is Dixon's explanation for the difficulty of producing a phylogeny for the languages of Australia; in sharp contrast to Indo-European or Polynesian, which are the daughters of relatively recent demographic expansion, the languages of the Aborigines are the product of many small societies at equilibrium for millennia.

Dixon's distinction between equilibria and punctuations cannot sensibly be interpreted as applying to single societies. It is not the case that communities are completely unchanging for millennia, and then suddenly undergo upheaval. All speech communities are fluctuating all the time, with their languages evolving, rising to dominance, or atrophying at the expense of neighbouring varieties. The idea of equilibrium is better seen as a property of a population of languages. Within the languages of, say, Australia, between AD 700 and 1700, no doubt every single language would have undergone a complex trajectory of wax and wane, but it may be the case that the average number of languages stayed around the same, and the rates of both extinction and glottogenesis were low relative to the number of languages. In this case, we can say that the whole system was at equilibrium, even though none of its component parts was. This is a dynamic, statistical interpretation of equilibrium similar to that applied to a gas in physics. A gas can be at equilibrium if its pressure and volume are unchanging; this does not mean that the individual molecules within it are still, but rather that their activity sums to zero.[1]

The weakness of Dixon's approach is that of most typologies of history; it imposes a discrete dichotomy on an underlying continuum. Once one looks closely at the historical record, it is hard to say where the equilibria end and the punctuations begin. A historical event (say the displacement of the Moriori by the Maori on the Chatham Islands in the South Pacific in 1835) may look like a punctuation at one spatial scale—it certainly was for the Moriori—but seem no more than a stochastic fluctuation when seen at another. In truth there are not two qualitatively different kinds of historical change, one that occurs during punctuation and one that is characteristic of equilibrium. There is just history. Similarly, it is probably simplistic to postulate that the mode of language change will be ramification in punctuations and diffusion in equilibria. Both are going on all the time, though their relative strengths vary. Similar comments to these can be applied to the biological theory from which Dixon draws inspiration—the punctuated equilibrium model of evolution (Eldredge and Gould 1972). Though there may be periods during which evolution is for some reason especially rapid, there is nothing qualitatively different about these periods compared to others, and the mechanism of change is still just ordinary Darwinism (Dennett 1995).

Despite these problems, Dixon's (1997) contribution is extremely useful, at least as a heuristic. It is useful for historical linguistics, because it serves as a reminder that ramification is not the only mode of change, and that the proportion of change that is treelike is not a constant but rather varies with non-linguistic circumstances. It is useful for linguistic prehistory, because it supplies a crude framework for relating the prehistory of languages to other aspects of prehistory. This remains true even if we accept the point that the distinction between equilibrium and punctuation is one of degree rather than kind.

I will, then, adopt the vocabulary of punctuation and equilibrium in considering the evolution of language diversity through time. The first long equilibrium we can identify was that of the Palaeolithic, of hunters and gatherers before the origin of farming. This equilibrium lasted upwards of 40,000 years and perhaps much more. The first great linguistic punctuation, at least in the Old World, was

---

[1] This is usually the interpretation of equilibrium Dixon (1997: 68–73) has in mind, but he could be clearer on this important point. Sometimes he seems to imply that individual societies in equilibrium periods are harmonious, particularly in the sense of unassertive. For example, '[in equilibrium there would be] a number of groups living in relative harmony with each other, each more or less . respecting their neighbours and their neighbours' ideas and religion. . . . Decisions on what a village or kinship group should do would be reached by consensus, with some senior members of the group guiding the discussion . . . [conflict would be limited] by a tacit understanding not to go too far' (Dixon 1997: 78). This Rousseauesque picture is anthropologically naïve, as a brief reading of Keeley (1996) or Edgerton (1992) will reveal. The lack of military dominance of any one group in such areas as New Guinea or Aboriginal Australia has more to do with demographic weakness, technological limitations, and inability to command economic surpluses than any pacific cultural attributes. I am indebted to Lyle Campbell for discussion of this point.

the beginning of the Neolithic, after which an equilibrium was reached in some parts of the globe. The early stages of European colonial expansion, I will argue, were just a tragic and delayed aftershock of the Neolithic punctuation. Finally, the second great punctuation involved the rise of expansionist industrial economies; I will conclude by suggesting that we cannot at present predict what equilibrium will be reached after this punctuation has done its work. This periodization of history is clearly simplistic, and no doubt there have been many more local perturbations and trajectories, but in a book such as this one we are concerned only with the main worldwide patterns.

5.2. The Palaeolithic Equilibrium

We cannot say when human language arose in its present form, but we can set some limits. The expansion of modern humans into greater Australia was underway 50,000 years ago (Roberts *et al.* 1990). Australians were then isolated from the Eurasian and African populations for most of their history. Yet Australians have exactly the same linguistic abilities as everyone else; it follows that, whatever the biological prerequisites for language are, they were in place no later than 50,000 years ago. They had probably been in place for a substantial time before; there is no real evidence for the view that language evolved suddenly or only 50,000 years ago. However, we can take this as a date by which we can be absolutely sure that language already existed in fully modern form. I will thus take it as the sure beginning of what I shall call the Palaeolithic equilibrium.

Over the Palaeolithic, humans gradually filled up the world from their probable African homelands. As well as establishing early habitation in all of Africa and the Near East, they pushed north and east into Asia, and north-west into Europe. New Guinea and Australia were settled by 50,000 BP, as we have seen, and the Americas were finally reached across the Bering Strait from Siberia, probably between 20,000 and 12,000 years ago. The spread down through the Americas from Alaska to the southern tip was completed relatively quickly once this threshold had been crossed. Thus the whole of the presently inhabited world was peopled by hunting and gathering societies, except for far northern latitudes, and most of the Pacific islands, which were settled in a Neolithic expansion from 2000 BC.

Neolithic societies—those based on farming and herding—did not appear anywhere until around 10,000 years ago. Thus the period of hunting and gathering was the single longest period of human history, at least 50,000 years in Europe, Asia, and Australia, longer in Africa, and 10,000–20,000 years in the Americas. Only a few countries, such as New Zealand, had no such period at all.

The probable language diversity of the Palaeolithic period can be partly inferred from ethnographic patterns. We saw in Chapter 4 that the size of ethnolinguistic communities of hunter-gatherers is generally smaller than that of communities of farmers living in similar habitats. Although farming groups can be very small where ecological conditions permit, as in New Guinea, as ecological risk increases, the average size of their groups also increases. With hunter-gatherers, the pattern does not seem to hold.

Our one model for the Palaeolithic situation, as we have already seen, is that of Australia, where the whole continent had a pure hunting and gathering economy from first settlement until European contact. In Section 4.8 it was argued that community size across pre-colonial Australia was fairly uniform, and we estimated that the ratio of people to languages was between about 1000:1 and 3000:1 (266 languages; population estimates 251,000–750,000). Ethnographic evidence suggests that hunter-gatherer societies are never very much bigger than this; in the range of a few hundred to a few thousands, but never in the high tens or hundreds of thousands. This is much smaller than the average size of a farming group; thus there would have been many more languages relative to the size of the population in the Palaeolithic. Whether there would have been more languages in absolute terms is unclear, since the population in the Palaeolithic was much smaller than that of the Neolithic. I return to this question below.

The reasons that hunter-gatherer societies are so much smaller are twofold. First, they utilize a much broader range of resources than agriculturalists, who devote much of their time to the specialized nurture of a few plant or animal species. This means that they can deal with ecological fluctuations by changing their foraging patterns rather than having to develop large networks of exchange. The corollary of their lack of specialization is that, since the resources they use occur only with their natural abundance and are not deliberately husbanded, they cannot support high local densities of people, as this would quickly exhaust the food supply.

Secondly, hunter-gatherers respond to local resource shortages primarily by mobility. Thus, where resources are seasonally unavailable, they move, and their movement is even less constrained than that of specialized herders. Where resources are locally depleted by population pressure, once again, the primary response is through mobility. This means that individual hunter-gatherer societies never increase greatly in terms of numbers of members. The territory they occupy varies in size, being rather small where resources are rich, such as on the northern coasts of Australia, and the Pacific north-west of the United States, and much larger in arid environments. As they grow numerically and begin to overexploit their local resources, though, they repeatedly fission and move into new territory. This pattern presumably explains the gradual filling-up of the world during the Palaeolithic. In response to local depletion of game and wild foods, groups moved ever outward into virgin space, filling all of Africa, eventually traversing all of Asia into greater Australia, and all of the Americas from Alaska to Patagonia.

Repeated fission and expansion represents, I assume, a perfectly adaptive strategy through a period where population densities were low, the ecological conditions were favourable, and game and resources were available. The conclusion that agriculture and denser settlement would have been better for Palaeolithic societies but they were not yet advanced enough to invent that is to be avoided; hunter-gatherer societies were generally healthier, through a broader diet, and possibly less hard-worked than early farmers. The numerous instances of societies reverting from farming to hunting and gathering confirm the general conclusion, though, that the different systems should be seen not as stages on a ladder of progress from primitive to advanced, but as alternative food-procuring strategies, each of which has certain advantages and disadvantages and is suited to different environments (Layton *et al.* 1991).

If we take the view that Palaeolithic history consisted, broadly speaking, of repeated fission and spread, then the implications for language diversity are clear. The number of languages would have risen in broadly linear relation to the size of the human population. If we can estimate the population size, then we can even estimate the number of languages over time, by using the Australian figure of 1,000–3,000 people per language.

Estimating prehistoric population size is fraught with assumptions and difficulty. The most thorough attempt is by Hassan (1981: ch. 12), who bases his conclusions on a consideration of the total settled area at different times, and an archaeological model of hunter-gatherer population densities. Hassan estimates a world population of 1.2 million in the Middle Palaeolithic (70,000 BP), rising to 6 million in the Upper Palaeolithic and between 8 million and 9 million on the eve of the Neolithic. These figures agree, within the huge margins of error we must accord to such estimates, with Biraben's (1979) figure of around half a million people 40,000 years ago, expanding to 5 million with the expansions of that time, and remaining around that level until the onset of the Neolithic.

Thus our Palaeolithic estimates give us a pre-farming world population of the order of between 5 million and 9 million people. Assuming the Australian ratio of people to languages gives the late Palaeolithic global language diversity as between 1,667 and 9,000 languages.

Clearly these estimates have no pretension to accuracy, but they are interesting speculations. The number of living languages now, in the afterglow of the Neolithic, is around 6,500 (Chapter 4), a figure that has certainly declined in the last 500 years. Relative to the number of people alive, the number of languages in the late Palaeolithic was vastly greater than that in the Neolithic. In absolute terms, however, the estimates suggest it was in the same range as the present. This is perhaps not so surprising; farming communities may contain many times more people than their hunter-gatherer equivalents, but their population densities tend to be ten or 100 times as great (Hassan 1981). The number of languages fitting into the world's space might, therefore, have been much the same for a long period under both conditions. The Neolithic revolution did, however, eventually and indirectly, cause a further punctuation, which did and still is greatly decreasing the world's language diversity. The events of the Neolithic are the subject of the next section.

5.3. The Neolithic Punctuation

Shifts from hunting and gathering to the specialized husbandry of plants and animals occurred independently in several continents. The earliest confirmed dates are around 8,500 BC in western Asia. The western Asian farming complex involved wheat, barley, sheep, and goats, and was to spread to North Africa, northern India, and Europe in time. A separate farming transition, based on rice and millet, was underway in China by 7500 BC. This complex, and especially the cultivation of rice, was destined to push inland in China, south into south-east Asia, and into the islands of the Near Pacific.

The earliest transition to farming outside Eurasia was probably the onset of New Guinean horticulture based on sugar cane and bananas, which may date from 7000 BC, though the intensive highland farming of such groups as the Enga in New Guinea is a later development stemming from after the introduction of sweet potato from the Americas. There are three major traditional farming complexes in Africa, though the extent to which their origins were independent of each other and of those in Eurasia is still a matter of some debate. A cereal (sorghum)-based complex is found along the southern fringes of the Sahara desert, where the environment is seasonally arid. This is the system of the Hausa described in Section 4.4.2, and it had developed by 5000 BC. A separate complex, based on yams and suited to the lush equatorial environments of central Africa, had arisen, probably in Cameroon, by 3000 BC. Finally, the Ethiopian seasonal crops teff and coffee may represent a separate development from the western Asian and other African complexes.

Agriculture seems to have arisen in at least three places in the Americas independently from each other; in Central America based on maize and beans by 3500 BC, in tropical South America, probably around the same time but using manioc, and the eastern USA by 2500 BC in a complex based on sunflowers, sumpweed, and a seed-bearing plant called goosefoot.

The reasons for the multiple appearances of farming are not entirely understood. Earlier schools of thought assumed the unconditional superiority of farming as a means of procuring a living, and were therefore forced to the conclusion that Palaeolithic societies were unable to make the transition, perhaps owing to excessively primitive technology. Such approaches of course provide no explanation as to why the right technologies did arise when and where they did, and cannot account for instances of reversion to hunting and gathering. Furthermore, they do not recognize the costs of the transition to agriculture. Archaeological evidence shows that early farming communities suffered sharp increases in the rate of infectious diseases, which stem from the sanitary and epidemiological consequences of the increased crowding-together of people with other people and with domestic animals (Cohen 1994; Diamond 1997). Skeletal evidence also suggests much poorer nutrition than in pre-farming societies, through a decline in dietary diversity and quality (Cohen 1994).

More sophisticated analyses stress both the costs and benefits of farming, and assume that the shift will occur when these change relative to the costs and benefits of hunting and gathering. Most models assume that farming, which is the specialized husbanding of low-value resources, arose in response to the local depletion of higher-value wild alternatives. The causes of such depletion may have been climatic change (Layton *et al.* 1991), or population pressure (Cohen 1977). Diamond (1997) also stresses that the available range of suitable plant and animal species for domestication is also very variable from place to place, and so the benefits of agriculture depend on the local biogeography.

Whatever the precise causes of agricultural origins, their effects are fairly clear, and, though they were far from all beneficial, they guaranteed the spread of farming. As we have seen, increases in infectious disease and a decline in dietary quality entailed an increase in mortality. However, agriculture and sedentism also allowed fertility to rise so sharply that the increase in mortality was outweighed, and the rate of population growth increased, fairly quickly reaching a level around 100 times greater than that which had been typical (Hassan 1981: 125).

The result of this increased rate was that farming populations spread out from their original centres in waves of advance, as their populations grew and thus occupied more space (Ammerman and Cavalli-Sforza 1973). Hunter-gatherer societies at the fringes of such expansions found their habitats occupied by denser and more numerous farming populations, whose activities made their traditional subsistence untenable. They were either assimilated, killed, or driven before the advancing wave. The progress of such waves would not have been entirely implacable or constant; the two economies coexisted in several regions (Zvelebil and Zvelebil 1988), often in symbiosis, and some habitats were more appropriate for farming than others. None the less, the transition to agriculture clearly initiated a major punctuation in human geography.

The expanding wave of first farmers and herders carried language with it in numerous instances. As we shall see in the next chapter, many of the world's largest and most familiar language families may well have been spread out in this way. Innumerable small languages of hunting and gathering communities would have disappeared under the Neolithic advance, which was probably the first mass extinction of languages. However, as I argued in the previous section, over the long term the total number of languages spoken may not have decreased. As the farming communities became established, they split up into units whose size depended on ecological and geographical conditions, and diversification began again.

The origin of agriculture, then, immediately entailed a replacement of some languages by others. This has important implications for phylogenetic diversity, as we shall see in the next chapter, though it may have left the amount of language diversity about the same for several thousand years. However, it was eventually to have enormous implications for language diversity, for post-Neolithic history took very different courses in different parts of the world. It is to these trajectories and their consequences that we now turn.

5.4. The Neolithic Aftershock

As we have seen, agriculture developed independently in China, western Asia, sub-Saharan Africa, New Guinea, and at least three places in the Americas. Its effects were rather different in each continent. By historical times, farming had spread to cover all of Eurasia except the far north and small pockets of Indian and south-east Asian rainforests, and population growth was rapid across the continent. In Africa, the yam-based farming complex had spread to cover the tropical part of the continent by AD 500, alternating with herding where the environment favoured that activity. Hunting and gathering only remained in pockets between the different agricultural complexes—in areas such as the middle belt of West Africa, sandwiched between yam-based equatorial farmers and cereal-based Sahelian farmers—and in encapsulated pockets such as the pygmies of the Congo and the San of Botswana. Africa's rate of population increase, however, remained lower than that of Eurasia. In New Guinea, agriculture was not intensive, and it coexisted with hunting and gathering for thousands of years. Population densities remained low, except in the Highlands above 2,500 metres where a large, expanding population dependent on intensive farming developed after the introduction of the sweet potato. In the Americas, the three agricultural centres remained circumscribed, and large parts of the continent were still hunting and gathering within the last 300 years. In Australia, agriculture did not develop at all.

These different trajectories assured that the rates of population expansion in the different continents were divergent. Over 10,000 years even a modest divergence in growth rates produces quite stark results. By the time of Christ, Biraben (1979: 15) estimates that the world population was around 252 million. Of these, 227 million (which is 90 per cent) were in Eurasia and North Africa, with just 12 million (5 per cent) in sub-Saharan Africa, 12 million in the Americas (5 per cent), and less than one million in Australia and the Pacific (less than 1 per cent). By 1750, Biraben puts the population of Eurasia and North Africa at 646 million, whilst that of the Americas was still just 18 million, and that of Australia and the Pacific 3 million.

The ultimate causes of these huge differences are a matter of debate. Diamond (1997) attributes the Eurasian demographic advantage to a chance combination of, first, a superior suite of plant and animal species to domesticate, and, secondly, a large, open east–west axis along which this suite could spread. Whatever the causes, the consequences have dramatically altered the world's linguistic diversity.

Under the conditions of high population growth and density of Eurasia and North Africa, a number of huge languages eventually evolved. These were backed up by states that teemed with people sufficiently to have armies and bureaucracies, and also by writing. Such factors enabled them to spread far beyond the typical social networks of an agrarian community. The official languages of most modern nation states are Eurasian languages that evolved this way—Arabic, Chinese, English, French, Spanish, and so on. All of the twenty languages with the most speakers today are Eurasian in origin, if we admit Indonesian and Arabic as Eurasian languages. Under constant pressure for more space, the speakers of the big Eurasian and North African languages also invested in technologies of long-distance transport and large-scale warfare, which eventually allowed them to expand beyond their own shores.

The centres of highest growth and cultural expansionism within Eurasia have shifted repeatedly through history. In the west of the continent, the centre has moved from the Middle East and the Levant, where both agriculture and urbanism began, to the Nile Valley and later to Europe (Abu-Lughod 1989). Such shifts have often been provoked by environmental degradation, or local population crashes provoked by disease or famine. In the east, the centre has consistently remained in the Yangtze and Yellow river valleys of China.

By the second millennium after Christ, pressure to expand beyond Eurasia had become intense, especially along the densely populated seaboards of the land mass. China led the way in the technologies of such expansion, and by the fifteenth century it was sending huge fleets of large, well-armed sailing ships as far afield as India and East Africa. For reasons that remain slightly mysterious, the voyages of these fleets were suspended after 1433, and the impetus for Eurasian expansion shifted to the western coast of the continent (Crosby 1986: 106; Abu-Lughod 1989).

Expansionary movement from Europe had been suppressed by the Black Death of the mid-fourteenth century, which killed perhaps one-third of the population (Crosby 1986: 52). By the 1450s the population was expanding rapidly once again (Braudel 1985: 33), and by around 1490 the pressure to expand had become acute, whilst maritime technology had also advanced. In 1487 Bartholmeu Diaz rounded the southern tip of Africa, and in 1492 Columbus reached the Americas. Between 1519 and 1522 Magellan completed the circumnavigation of the world, and colonial expansion had begun in earnest.

The subsequent historical events have been well recounted by numerous historians. Over 400 years, Europeans spread out to occupy much of the rest of the world, taking with them their livestock, their crops, their weeds and pests, and, of course, their languages. As Crosby (1986) has argued, the areas where Europeans were to settle were largely dictated by ecology and demography. Other parts of Eurasia were already densely settled, so they could not be easily appropriated. Thus there were never major European settlements of China or India. The Old World tropics had two great drawbacks. First, they were unsuited to the seasonal, cereal-based agriculture that formed the basis of the expanding way of life. Secondly, they were home to numerous equatorial diseases to which Europeans had had no exposure and to which they therefore had little resistance. Colonies in such areas as equatorial Africa and New Guinea had such high rates of mortality that they became known as 'white man's graves'.

The areas where settlements did take place in numbers were those of temperate latitude (in either hemisphere) and broadly European climate. This explains why there are societies of European descent in Australia and New Zealand but not New Guinea, South Africa but not the Congo, Argentina and the United States but not Ecuador. This process was really no more than the final playing-out at a global level of the waves of agricultural expansion that had begun at the Neolithic transition. A complex of people, plants, animals, and culture from a dense area were pushing into less saturated habitats, and destroying indigenous diversity as they went.

The European expansion had a devastating effect on the indigenous languages of the settled areas. Expanding European populations, whatever their rhetoric, had little interest in sharing the lands they were appropriating with anyone, and either murdered indigenous peoples, forcibly assimilated them, or drove them into marginal habitats that they could not use. Their replacement of the indigenous peoples was aided and abetted by allies that the European settlers had no idea they had, in the form of the micro-organisms that cause infectious diseases.

Australia and the Americas, as we have seen, did not have the high population densities of Eurasia, and also lacked domesticated livestock. Their populations therefore had no exposure to the major diseases that thrive under the dense packing of humans and their animals, such as smallpox, typhoid, measles, influenza, diphtheria, certain kinds of tuberculosis, bubonic plague, malaria, and yellow fever. No exposure meant no resistance, and so these diseases spread rapidly and devastatingly through indigenous populations as soon as contact with European carriers had been made. Estimates of the proportion of indigenes of the Americas and the Caribbean who died from infectious diseases before the populations eventually rallied vary from 50 per cent to 90 per cent (Kunitz 1994: 302). The Australians fared little better. Smallpox epidemics that began as soon as the first British settlement was established at Sydney in 1788 depopulated the immediate area and went on to ravage the continent. Through the nineteenth century, smallpox may have killed one-third of all indigenous Australians (Crosby 1986: 206).

Where indigenous populations did not die out, they were forcibly disrupted, and both disruption and reduction of numbers prevented them from continuing as viable cultural units. The effect of these processes on language diversity has proved devastating. Of the 266 or so Australian languages at the time of contact, thirty-two are listed as actually dead in Grimes (1993). Of the 234 that are listed as still spoken, thirty had one elderly speaker at the time of the census, and another 100 had fewer than ten speakers. Dixon (1997: 143), who may have more up-to-date information, suggests that 100 languages are now extinct, with another 100 heading towards extinction, with only around twenty being passed on to children at all.

The situation for the New World is much the same. Most of the languages of tropical South America and the Caribbean are long gone, and, as we saw in Chapter 4, the diversity of these areas is much lower than that of other equatorial areas that did not go through this punctuation. Central America has some larger and more resilient languages, but also many that are on the path to extinction. Finally, in North America, most of the languages have hung on into the late twentieth century, but they are spoken in much reduced communities, and, most importantly, few languages are being passed on to new generations.

The Neolithic itself, within the several continents where it occurred, entailed the loss of many languages before a flooding demographic, biological, and cultural tide. The process of Eurasian expansion I have called the Neolithic aftershock had the same effect, but there is a crucial difference between the two events in terms of their long-term effect on language diversity. In the Neolithic proper, the expanding farming communities gradually fragmented into small units, and their languages began to diverge, in time producing many new languages, perhaps as many languages as had been destroyed. In the Neolithic aftershock, however, it seems that almost no new languages have been created. This is because, by the time the Neolithic aftershock began, the expanding languages were backed up with writing and vastly improved technologies of communication and transportation, which allowed them to preserve an approximate coherence despite covering vast areas.

5.5. The Industrial Punctuation

The Neolithic aftershock—the expansion of Eurasian farmers into the rest of the temperate world—decimated or is decimating the language diversity of the Americas and Australia. There are many areas, however, that are high in language diversity and were not really affected. New Guinea, island south-east Asia, and most of sub-Saharan Africa were unsuitable for Eurasian settlement, and though they came under the political domination of European powers, their populations were never swamped in the way native Americans were, and they never went through demographic collapse.

The language diversity of those areas is now threatened, however, as is the diversity of small languages within Eurasia itself. This is because another punctuation, distinct from the Neolithic aftershock in its causes and its manner of operating, is coming hard on the heels of the previous one. I call this, for want of a more exact term, the industrial punctuation.

The industrial punctuation is, as we shall see, loosely associated with the industrial revolution and the change in life styles and living standards associated with it. It has involved populations speaking smaller languages staying where they are, but shifting, often rather gradually, to a larger language associated with a more developed economy. Thus the industrial punctuation is a spread of languages without a major spread of peoples. In this it differs markedly from the Neolithic punctuations, which involved the spread of languages and peoples together. Most of the languages disappearing in the industrial punctuation are not dying because their speakers are killed off wholesale or displaced from where they are; indeed, the populations involved are often increasing rapidly, but adopting a different tongue as they do so. The industrial punctuation has been going on for at least 500 years (which is why I say its association with the industrial revolution is only a loose one), but its pace has greatly quickened in the last 100 years, and at the end of the twentieth century there are probably fewer than twenty languages in the world that are not losing some of their ground because of it.

The dense population and productive agricultural complexes of Eurasia had many effects, one of which, as we have seen, was that Eurasians and especially Europeans set out in great numbers to occupy the vacant agricultural spaces of the planet. Another effect within those societies was a sustained trend of improvement in agricultural productivity, increasing commerce, and spread of technology, which was certainly well under way, sporadically perhaps, by the late Middle Ages (Gimpel 1976). This slow increase worked up to a dramatic and irreversible transformation of life styles after 1760, when the industrial revolution, as conventionally defined, began in Great Britain. The trajectory of European economies became quite different after the industrial revolution; incomes for many people were transformed from something that could be expected to fluctuate with the years and seasons but not change over the generations to something that can reasonably be expected to increase dramatically over a single lifetime—as they have, broadly speaking, for every generation of Western Europeans this century. Life expectancy was significantly increased in early seventeenth century Europe, not so much because of modern medicine as because of higher real incomes leading to better food and housing (Lane 1978: ch. 1). Age at first reproduction also decreased, and Western European populations began a boom that would have been as significant as the Neolithic transition for world population if it were not for the peculiar phenomenon of demographic transition, which means that people in industrial societies have tended to voluntarily limit their reproduction.

One school of historical thought, traceable to Engels and to the English historian Toynbee, has sought to emphasize the negative consequences of industrialization on human well-being, and, of course, all social transformation, whether to farming or to industry, has costs as well as benefits, losers as well as winners. None the less, the evidence is clear enough that, overall, industrialization has meant better life expectancies and health, higher incomes with which to procure a range of goods and services, and a greater range of economic choices for most people. The development of the industrialized economy has, however, been geographically patchy, with areas of concentration adjacent to areas that are still underdeveloped, and this patchiness is crucial in understanding the language shifts associated with industrialization.

The general pattern has been for people in an underdeveloped area to come to associate the cultural and economic prestige of a developed area with the language of that area, and so begin adopting that language. Kulick (1992) gives a classic example of this from the New Guinea village of Gapun, where the national language Tok Pisin has come to be associated with access to modern goods and education, whilst the vernacular Taiap expresses backwardness. The same dynamic had been played out over 100 years earlier in the British Isles. For many Welsh, Irish, Manx, Cornish, and Scots Gaelic speakers, their mother tongues had come to be 'rustic, stagnant . . . familiar, emotional and comic' (Gregor 1980: 302), whilst English was perceived as the language of the future. An Ulster speaker of Irish was to admit as late as 1951 that, 'for some, Irish is synonymous with poverty and social inferiority'.

In both the contemporary Third World cases such as that described by Kulick (1992), and the historical cases closer at home, a classic pattern is established. It begins with a monolingual or nearly monolingual community. An ambitious younger generation that has contact with, or at least aspiration to, the more developed economy becomes bilingual in the language of that economy and the vernacular. Their children, the third generation, then become monolingual in the dominant language. For them, not only has the vernacular lost its prestige in relation to the larger language, but much of the functional need for it has been attenuated by the fact that the generation above them is all bilingual. This pattern can take longer or shorter periods to play out in different places, but its effect is usually the same; the dominant language becomes primary and the vernacular is forgotten.

Whether speakers of minority languages are right to associate the languages of the developed economies with the economic possibilities of those economies, which they understandably desire, is a difficult question, but this perception has certainly become widespread in many parts of the world. It has been abetted in no small measure by the cultural and political élites of the developed economies, who have typically owned the media, dominated institutions, and been keen to see their cultural stock rise. What is clear is that the industrial punctuation has sent a number of large languages expanding like cultural juggernauts across the world.

The first casualties of the industrial punctuation were the British Celtic languages, small rural tongues on the fringes of the first developed economy. In the late Middle Ages the Celtic languages covered much of the British Isles; most of Scotland, all of Ireland, Cornwall, the Isle of Man, and not just Wales but English counties bordering Wales such as Herefordshire and Gloucestershire (Durkacz 1983: 210). As the English economy became more powerful, those communities on the boundary between the English- and Celtic-speaking areas began to be drawn into it. The three-generation pattern of language shift was established, and as a result a moving frontier of English and Celtic was established, with Celtic always retreating. Welsh was pushed westward into its current heartlands. Irish was pushed westward by an English frontier that started around Dublin and pushed almost to the Atlantic coast, so that by the mid-twentieth century Irish hung on as a first language only in some far western pockets and islands. Gaelic retreated north and west into the highlands and islands of Scotland. Finally, Manx and Cornish disappeared as spoken languages before any modern revival could really begin. Towns were always ahead of the countryside in this shift, as their populations had more contact and communication with the English economy.

The relative contributions of English political oppression, on the one hand, and active socio-economic choice *for* English by Celtic speakers, on the other, have been hotly debated and will no doubt continue to be so (Hindley 1990, Durkacz 1983; see, more generally, Ladefoged 1992, Dorian 1993), though in fact these two are not either/or alternatives (Nettle and Romaine, forthcoming: ch. 6). Clearly, the precise events and locally important factors are extremely complex, and require more detailed discussion than can be given here. None the less, the clearest pattern to emerge from the Celtic case is that post-industrial language shift involves an extreme form of the major force in language change that we have already discussed, namely social selection. I argued in Chapters 2 and 3 that speakers will choose the linguistic variants associated with the groups they identify with and aspire to belong to. The same applies when the choice is between two whole languages. Local vernaculars have enormous benefits in terms of in-group solidarity, and these benefits have kept distinct ethnic languages in place for centuries on the fringes of much larger languages. However, when a very large discrepancy arose between the social or economic opportunities available in one community and those in the other, people tended to make a social selection for the whole package of the developed culture, including its language.

The cultural-economic juggernaut that pushed the Celtic languages to the fringes of the British Isles has never paused since. As contact with developed economies intensifies all over the world, the languages of those economies—English, French, Spanish, Russian—are spreading rapidly through Eurasia, parts of Africa, New Guinea, and the residual indigenous communities of the Americas and Oceania, and small languages are disappearing under their spread. Sometimes the spreading language is not one of the languages of the most developed economies, but a medium-sized local language that has come to be seen as higher in terms of economic opportunity and prestige than the vernacular. Examples of such languages are Hausa in West Africa, Swahili in East Africa, Tagalog in the Phillippines, and Tok Pisin in New Guinea. Whether these languages will in the end prove to be merely the shock troops for an ultimate invasion by English and French is as yet impossible to say.

The local politics of language shift (and the prospects for halting it, to which I return below) are very different in different areas. In particular, the balance of coercion and choice involved, in so far as those two things can be objectively identified, is variable. The topic of language death is surely the most important in linguistic anthropology today, and it deserves a much fuller and more nuanced treatment, which we hope to present elsewhere (Nettle and Romaine, forthcoming). None the less, the pattern of shift seems sufficiently widespread to talk of a single process—the industrial punctuation, as I have called it—without absurdity. We should note, too, that, in a few places like Australia, the Neolithic aftershock and the industrial punctuation came so much together that they cannot really be prised apart in any discussion of language death. This does not change the overall utility of identifying two different punctuations.

5.6. Prospect

We have seen, then, that there is a worldwide crisis under way in the maintenance of language diversity. Languages have been periodically killed off—by the Neolithic, and by the European expansion of 500–200 years ago—through history, but this crisis seems particularly grave. The unknowns are so great that speculation on the ultimate outcome of the crisis is difficult. Curiosity, though, forces us to give at least some consideration to what may happen.

I argued in the previous section that the latest waves of language death can be attributed to two things: first, the universal mechanism of social selection in language, and, secondly, the large disparities in economic opportunity that exist between the world's different peoples. Now the universality of the first of these, and the hugeness of the second, might seem to suggest that the spread of the developed-world languages is unstoppable and the only conceivable future equilibrium is that in which there are only one or two languages. This position is perhaps unnecessarily gloomy. Vernacular languages have enormous appeal in terms of local solidarity, as we have seen, and there is some evidence that where there is real economic development, which reduces the economic disparities which underlie language shift, people tend to become interested in vernacular languages again, and may derive great prestige from them. They may then find a 'middle way' of bilingualism in a vernacular language and a language of wider communication.

Coupled with this possibility are more tolerant attitudes and great improvements in the affordability of technology. Whereas previously producing a book required a printing works, compositors, and metal type specially cut for the language to be printed, it now requires no more than a computer, a printer, and a photocopier. Tapes and audio discs can now be cut for almost nothing; small magazines can be circulated at low cost; and cable television and the internet allow for more diversity and specificity in local communication. The facilities are therefore in place for a far greater plurality of voices in the language market place, and so, where there is demand for vernacular culture, it can be more easily supplied.

These developments may give heart to those who wish to support medium-sized languages in Europe or North America. For many languages, however, they will probably make no difference. Many languages, particularly in the Third World, are either so small, or spoken by communities whose economies are so disadvantaged, that shift is likely to be rapid and total in the rush for development.

The median number of speakers for all the languages of the world is just 5,000.[2] Crude size is not the only determinant of language viability; a group of 500 could be maintained in Papua New Guinea, but not in Western Europe. None the less, we can use speaker statistics to make some ballpark projections.

Table 5.1 shows the proportion of languages in each continent of the world with fewer than various benchmark numbers of speakers. This table allows us to draw several inferences. First, let us assume that languages with less than 150 speakers are in grave danger wherever they are. There are over 600 of these, 11.5 per cent of all the languages in the world. The proportion is much higher, however, throughout the Americas, Australia, and the Pacific. It is close to one-third of languages for these regions. If the languages smaller than 150 speakers are the most endangered, then mass extinction will bite much harder and sooner in the Americas and the Pacific than in Africa or Asia.

If the size required for medium-term safety is taken as 10,000 speakers, then 59.4 per cent of all languages will be lost in the medium term. If it is taken, perhaps more realistically, as 100,000 speakers, 83.8 per cent will die out, including virtually all of those of Australia and the Pacific. Africa and Asia, which have more medium-sized languages, will sustain much more diversity. If the safety level is taken as one million speakers, 95.2 per cent of all languages will be lost,

---

[2] These and subsequent statistics are from the numerical database from which the *Ethnologue* is compiled. Speaker statistics are available for 5,645 languages. Thus there are nearly 1,000 missing values. Note that international languages are assigned to the continent from which they originate. Thus the statement that there are no North American languages with more than one million speakers excludes English, Spanish, etc., which are treated as European for these purposes.

TABLE 5.1. *Percentages of languages in different continents and in the world as a whole having fewer than the indicated numbers of speakers*

Continent	<150	<1000	<10,000	<100,000	<1,000,000
Africa	1.7	7.5	32.6	72.5	94.2
Asia	5.5	21.4	52.8	81	93.8
Europe	1.9	9.9	30.2	46.9	71.6
North America	22.6	41.6	77.8	96.3	100
Central America	6.1	12.1	36.4	89.4	100
South America	27.8	51.8	76.5	89.1	94.1
Australia/Pacific	22.9	60.4	92.8	99.5	100
World	11.5	30.1	59.4	83.8	95.2

including every single language indigenous to North America, Central America, Australia, New Guinea, and the Pacific, plus almost all of those of South America.

These figures are just illustrative. The true pattern of language extinction will follow not from numbers of speakers of particular languages but from the patterns of costs, benefits, constraints, and opportunities that those speakers experience. None the less, the figures give some sense of the loss of language diversity that we may be about to go through. Most of our human heritage is disappearing before our eyes.

6 Phylogenetic Diversity

6.1. Introduction

In the previous two chapters we examined the distribution of language diversity across the globe and through time. In this chapter we shift attention to diversity at a different level, that of the family of languages. As I pointed out in Section 1.3, there is no necessary correlation between diversity of languages and diversity of language families. The Congo, for example, is rich in languages, but they are almost all closely related, belonging to the Bantu branch of the Niger-Congo. I will call diversity of higher-level units of this kind *phylogenetic diversity*.[1] This chapter first presents information on the distribution of the world's phylogenetic diversity, and then considers the kind of processes that have produced that distribution.

6.2. Lineages and Stocks

A phylogenetic grouping of languages is identifiable not just because there are shared items, which can also arise by diffusion, but because there are systematic equivalences across sets of items. Where there are regular sound correspondences between languages, and where whole morphological paradigms can be identified as cognate, the best explanation for the resemblance is that they descend continuously from some common ancestor, with some of their sound classes altered by shifts in the meantime.

Phylogenetic groupings can be identified at many levels, from sub-groups of one or two languages to vast families spanning half a continent. The languages of the Congo, for example, belong on one view to the successively wider groupings Narrow Bantu, Broad Bantu, Bantoid, Benue-Zambesi, South-Central Niger-Congo, Niger-Congo, and Niger-Kordofanian (Ruhlen 1987: 291–2). Following Nichols (1992: 25), I will use the term *lineage* to refer to phylogenetic groupings in general, at whatever level. As one moves up the scale from small lineages to large ones, the proportion of shared items and the clarity of the relationships decrease, and the very largest lineages proposed are generally controversial, as the

---

[1] Nichols (1990) calls this type of diversity *genetic diversity* and its density *genetic density*. I prefer to use the term *phylogenetic* where many linguists would use *genetic*, to avoid confusion with genetics in the sense of DNA.

relationships involved become very distant and alternative explanations in terms of diffusion of items or chance resemblance need to be considered.

To investigate the distribution of phylogenetic diversity, one needs to choose a reference level of lineage to count. Here we shall follow the best available surveys, those of Nichols (1990, 1992). Nichols investigates the diversity of lineage type she calls the *stock*. This she defines as the deepest phylogenetic node that is reconstructible by the standard comparative method of historical linguistics (Nichols 1990: 477; 1992: 24–5). Nichols does not claim that there are no higher-level nodes than the stock that might be identified; she is merely defining a comparable unit that is at the limit of what the comparative method can reconstruct. In fact, units of much greater depth than Nichols's stocks are usually controversial, though Nilo-Saharan and Niger-Congo are examples of such units that are widely accepted.

It is important to stress that stocks and other lineages of languages are of no significance to the people who speak them in the here and now. A person's social and geographical opportunities are affected by how many other people speak his language, as we have seen in the preceding chapters. It makes no difference to anyone, however, how many other languages there are in his language stock. The other languages of the stock will be, by definition, mutually unintelligible with his own, and this is enough to exclude him from them, whether they belong to the same lineage or not. In fact, few people have any idea what other languages their language is related to, whereas they often know very well who speaks their language. Stocks, then, like genera in biology, are merely units that we, as later observers, can identify traces of in contemporary distributions, and, like genera, they reflect not contemporary behaviour but past origins.[2]

6.3 The Distribution of Stocks

Nichols (1992: 233) has calculated the density of stocks (stocks per million square miles) for the whole world divided into ten continental and subcontinental areas.[3] For comparison I have calculated the language density for those areas as well, by summing the country data from Chapter 4. The data are given in Table 6.1.

Over the world, the language density of a region does not correlate with its phylogenetic density ($r_s = 0.5$, $n = 8$, n.s.), though New Guinea is highest on both. However, by plotting phylogenetic density against language density, as in Figure 6.1, a type of patterning becomes apparent.

[2] For this reason, Nichols's (1990: 498) argument that the Americas could not have been colonized by a group speaking a language isolate, because isolates cannot survive in high latitudes, makes no sense. There are many factors that could prevent people making the cold, difficult passage across the Bering Strait from Siberia to Alaska; whether their language was related to any others is not one of them.

[3] I have also excluded one of Nichols's ten geographical areas (the ancient Near East), since it consists only of dead languages.

TABLE 6.1. *Data on linguistic diversity for the nine continental and subcontinental areas of the world*

Area	Languages	Language density	Stocks	Phylogenetic density	Languages per stock
Africa	2,614	88.8	20	4.4	130.7
N. Eurasia	732	21.5	18	3.3	40.7
S. and SE Asia	1,998	110.4	10	3.8	199.8
Oceania	306	322.1	4	—	76.5
New Guinea	1,109	1,197.6	27	227.3	41.1
Australia	234	30.41	15	13.0	15.6
North America	243	12.3	50	16.9	4.9
Mesoamerica	381	144.2	14	71.7	27.2
South America	595	33.3	93	34.8	6.4

Note: Source for stocks and phylogenetic density is Nichols (1992), whose density figures have been converted from miles to kilometres. The density measures are units per million square kilometres. The language-density figures are obtained by summing the language counts for countries from Chapter 4. Languages spoken in several countries are thus counted several times, and so the figures, as absolute numbers of language in each continent, are inflated. However, this error affects each continent to about the same extent and so the figures remain useful for comparing continents.

In Figure 6.1 there are two groups of points. The first is the Old World (Africa, northern Eurasia, south and south-east Asia). Here the level of phylogenetic density is low, and the points are too few to ascertain whether increasing phylogenetic density is correlated with increasing language density, though the distribution is not inconsistent with this. The second group is everywhere else (the Americas, New Guinea, Australia). These areas have much more phylogenetic diversity for the same number of languages as the Old World. Furthermore, there are enough points for there to be a clear positive relationship between the two types of diversity; the more languages there are, the more language families there are ($r_s = 0.9$, $n = 5$, $p < 0.05$).

This, then, is the major global patterning in phylogenetic diversity at the stock level. The world separates into two zones: on the one hand, the Old World, and, on the other, what Nichols calls the Colonized Areas (New Guinea, Australia, the Americas).[4] Within each zone, the number of stocks is proportional to the number of languages present (clearly for the Colonized Areas, possibly for the Old World). However, the two zones are on different grades, the Colonized Areas having about an order of magnitude more stocks relative to their language diver-

[4] Oceania probably patterns with the Colonized Areas, though Nichols gives no phylogenetic density figure.

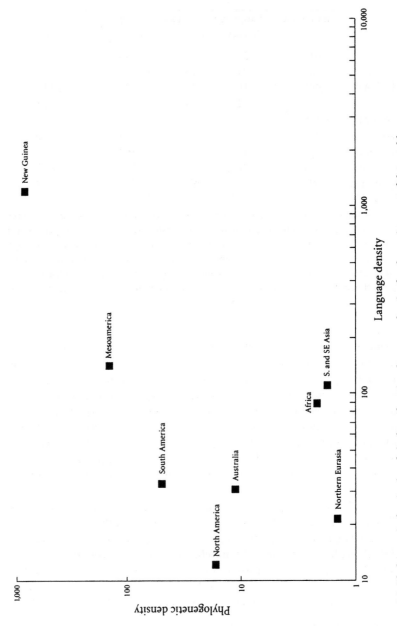

FIGURE 6.1. Phylogenetic density (stocks) plotted against language density for the main areas of the world
Source: Table 6.1.

sity than the Old World (the Old World has a total of 46 stocks to the Colonized Areas' 203). Looking at it the other way around, the Old World has an average of about ninety languages per stock, whilst the Colonized Areas have an average of about ten (Table 6.1, last column).

Various explanations could be put forward for the Old World/Colonized Area differences in stock diversity. We will consider two types of explanation in the next two sections. The first, suggested by Nichols (1990) herself, is that stock diversity is an increasing function of the time since founding of different continental populations. The second, to be considered in Section 6.5, is that the lower diversity of the Old World is a product of the Neolithic punctuations described in Chapter 5. Before embarking on these alternative explanations, however, it is worth considering whether the observed differences are linguistic realities or whether they are simply artefacts of our imperfect knowledge.

Nichols draws her list of stocks from the linguistic literature for each continent. There is no clear indication that all the stocks she identifies represent lineages of equal depth, for there is no easily available metric of distance between languages in a lineage that one could use to compare objectively. Nichols's choice of the units to count as stocks has no doubt been influenced by the scholarly consensus (such as there is) within each area, and there may be differences between continents in this respect. In Africa, for example, Greenberg's (1963) classification of all the languages into four large lineages has been extremely influential, despite the absence of comparative reconstruction for most of them (Dixon 1997: 32–5; Campbell 1998: 312–13). Of Greenberg's four lineages, Nichols counts only one, Afroasiatic, as a stock. For the rest, she takes the first-order branches as stocks (Nichols 1992: 283–4). None the less, her classification is undoubtedly informed by the influence of Greenberg (1963) on the subsequent literature. In the Americas, by contrast, a similar proposal to reduce all the languages to three large lineages (Greenberg 1987) has not met with wide acceptance, and has not much influenced subsequent literature, so the number of stocks identified remains large.

Now the difference in diversity between Africa and the Americas is probably a genuine one. The data and scholarship in both cases are sparse compared to what exists for Eurasia. Lack of sustained scholarship can have effects in either direction. It can lead to the acceptance of huge lineage proposals that represent in fact no more than areal convergence on a few visible features (as has been argued for Khoisan (Sands 1995)), leading to an underestimate of the number of stocks. It can also entail a failure to identify genuine phylogenetic units because the relevant reconstructions have not been done, leading to an overestimate of the number of stocks. The point is that lack of comparative work can lead to large uncertainties in the identification of lineages, and most of the world outside Europe suffers from such a lack.

These uncertainties should be borne in mind, then, when causes for the global distribution of stock diversity are sought. However, it seems from Figure 6.1 that the differences between the Old World and the Colonized Areas are both very large and rather systematic. Furthermore, the results of Nichols (1990) can be compared to those of other surveys of phylogenetic diversity. Dryer (1989) uses a shallower phylogenetic node, which he calls the *genus*, and comes up with 322 genera for the world as opposed to Nichols's 249 stocks. I have repeated all the calculations reported in this chapter using the density of Dryer's genera instead of Nichols's stocks and the results are largely the same. We can be reasonably confident, then, that the reported distribution reflects actual patterns in the world as far as we can grasp them at this time.

6.4. Stocks and Time: Nichols's Model

Nichols (1990: 503) suggests that stocks multiply linearly with time. The phylogenetic diversity of a linguistic population with no outside influence is thus a function of the time elapsed since that population started ramifying.[5] The context for this argument is a discussion of the settlement of the Americas. The languages of the Americas, excluding Eskimo and Na-Dene, which are more recent entries from Asia, form at least 140 stocks. Nichols argues that languages produce, on average, 1.6 descendant lineages every 5,000–8,000 years. Working backwards, she calculates that the time required to produce 140 stocks from a single ancestor at this rate is around 50,000 years. The settlement of the Americas, whether we accept Nichols's preferred date of 35,000 years ago or the more orthodox archaeological view of around 12,000 years ago, cannot have been 50,000 years ago, so Nichols thus urges us to conclude that the languages of the Americas stem from multiple colonizations and not a single ancestor.

It seems fair to note that Nichols's argument of a constant rate of ramification is only one of a suite of considerations she brings to bear on the problem of the settlement of the New World. It is, however, an extremely strange argument, for several reasons. First, the way in which the rate of 1.6 daughters per 5,000–8,000 years is arrived at is suspect. Nichols assumes that all of the units that she identifies as stocks have a time depth of 5,000–8,000 years. She has no independent evidence that this is right. In fact, linguists have no rigorous or widely accepted method of dating the split of phylogenetic groupings, and it is quite plausible to assume that the rate of diversification is actually rather variable

---

[5] I should note that Nichols does not believe that the number of stocks will multiply indefinitely; rather phylogenetic diversity will eventually reach an equilibrium level determined by geography. Her observations about the equilibrium level of diversity (Nichols 1990: 483–9) are actually more applicable to language diversity (see Chapter 4) than stock diversity, for which I find the idea of a time-free equilibrium level implausible. In any case, she implies that a vast period is necessary for the equilibrium to be reached.

(Dixon 1997: 46–9; Nettle, forthcoming *b*). Nichols's assumption about the time depth of stocks is thus quite unjustified.

Secondly, there is no principled reason at all for thinking that ramification should occur at some constant rate. The split of a language into several daughters occurs when some historical event, such as the movement of some of the people off into a new geographical niche, allows it. There is no reason to believe that such contingencies come along at anything like regular intervals. There could be dozens of opportunities for communities to split in just a few generations (as, for example, when the population growth rate is high and most of the land unin-habited—see below). At other times, a stagnant population, lack of new niches to live in, or geographical circumscription might mean no splits for millennia. The constant rate assumption cannot be justified.

Thirdly, and most importantly, data that are ably discussed by Nichols herself in the same paper (1990: 483–9) show that phylogenetic diversity in Eurasia and in Africa has actually been *reducing* for several millennia. This flatly contradicts any assumption that number of lineages increases linearly with time. Nichols might argue that the declining diversity of the Old World is rather untypical, being associated as it is with the rise and spread of Neolithic economies and then large empires, but large empires and farming transitions are as much a part of human history as anything else, and anyway there is no evidence for a more constant rate of ramification before they arose.

Nichols's own data simply fail to support her constant-rate assumption. The areas of longest human settlement (Africa, Eurasia) are, as Figure 6.1 shows and Nichols (1990: 486–8) herself observes, lower in diversity than those more recently settled. Thus, if there is a relationship between phylogenetic diversity and time, it is certainly not one of linear increase. In the next section, then, I will present an alternative model and consider possible explanations for the observed distribution of stocks.

6.5. Stocks and Time: An Alternative Model

When considering the probable relationship between phylogenetic diversity and time, it is useful to keep in mind Dixon's (1997) concepts of equilibrium and punctuation. The first great punctuation for any area would be its initial settlement. When humans first moved into a new area, the number of empty geographical niches available for them to live in would be extremely high. The population could thus fission repeatedly and often as new sub-groups moved out to fill these niches. Given the low population density, communicative isolation of these sub-groups would be common.

The breakthrough into a new continent, then, would be followed by a period of relatively rapid splitting and spreading as communities filled up the available niches of the new habitat. This is similar to the adaptive radiations of species seen in biological evolution when there are empty ecological niches; speciation is rapid until all the niches are filled, whereafter its rate declines.

The newly split languages would go on changing until they were sufficiently different to be identified as different families. After some more time had elapsed, they would be identified as different stocks, and so on. Once all the niches of the continent had been filled up, however, there would be little scope for further radiation of peoples or consequent ramification of languages. As Dixon (1997) argues, subsequent history would be dominated by a different kind of linguistic change. First, some groups might rise to local dominance through some demographic or technological advantage, and subsume other groups. Secondly, groups might intermarry, trade, or otherwise interact, leading to transfer of items between their languages and hence areas of linguistic convergence. Both of these events would become more frequent as the population of the continent increased and so groups packed tighter together.

This type of linguistic change would not produce much increase in the number of stocks over time. In fact, if anything, the apparent number of stocks would decrease. This could happen through extinction, as some peoples absorbed others, or through large scale areal convergence on certain linguistic items, which makes it difficult for subsequent linguists to identify the stock boundaries. Dixon (1997: 32–5) argues that such a process of convergence may account for some of the large Old World groupings of languages such as Niger-Kordofanian and Altaic, though these are still matters of debate.

We can produce a simple model of this situation as an alternative to Nichols's mode of linear increase in diversity. Let us begin with a continent containing one incoming lineage. Its rate of splitting would be not constant but density-dependent—that is, high when the continent is empty and there are many unoccupied niches, and slowing with time after that. We can model the production of stocks, then, by an equation against time of the form shown in (1),

$$\Delta S = A/t \qquad (1)$$

where ΔS is the number of new stocks produced, t is the time elapsed in thousands of years, and A is a constant reflecting the size of the land mass. We have to amend this equation slightly to allow for the fact that separate stocks are not produced overnight. Rather, it takes, according to Nichols (1992: 25), 5,000–8,000 years for sufficient evolutionary change to accrue for linguists to recognize two lineages as separate stocks. Ignoring for now the dubious assumptions that lie behind this figure, let us take its upper limit as the time delay required for new stocks to form. Thus the incoming stock remains unitary for 8,000 years, and so the time variable in Equation (1) must be lagged by this amount.

Now we must also incorporate the effects of stock extinction. Above, I argued that the disappearance of stocks will if anything increase as time goes by, owing to increased inter-group interaction and areal convergence. Here, we will assume for simplicity that stocks face a constant risk of extinction. If we set this at 5 per cent per thousand years (I make no claim that this is the real figure, and the precise value does not matter for what is to follow), then the number of extinctions in 1,000 years will be given by (2),

$$e = 0.05\ S \qquad (2)$$

where S is the total number of stocks.

We can use Equations (1) and (2) to track the total number of stocks, S, over time. The number of stocks at time point $t+1$ will be given by Equation (3).

$$S_{t+1} = S_t + \Delta S - e \qquad (3)$$

Starting with one stock, and taking the constant A as 70, the number of stocks over 100,000 years in a notional continent is shown in Figure 6.2. The figure shows the number of stocks rapidly rising to a maximum within 20,000 years, and then gradually falling as the rate of production of new stocks slows and extinction begins to bite. The Americas, with its high number of living stocks, looks very much as a continent in its first 20,000 years might be expected to look on the basis of this model.

The important point here is not the exact values of the model, which I have clearly handpicked to predict around 140 stocks after 12,000 years—my belief about the Americas—and for which I have no independent justification. The interest is the general shape of the curve, which will always be roughly the same, even if continental sizes and extinction probabilities are altered. This shape is clearly not one of ever-rising diversity. Even without incorporating the effects of the Neolithic and other punctuations, a simple, reasonable model predicts that the peak number of stocks should be reached quite soon after colonization, with a likely decline thereafter.

For greater realism, we should add the effects of subsequent punctuations to the model. The chief of these is the Neolithic transition discussed in Chapter 5. As we saw, the population increases associated with the transition to farming produce waves of advance of the farming peoples through previous hunter and gatherer territory. If the transition to agriculture occurs within one language group, then the language of that group will tend to spread in a wave as the group advances, subsuming many other languages and stocks as it goes.

Many of the large lineages we are familiar with have been spread as part of an economic punctuation in exactly this way (Renfrew 1987, 1991; Bellwood 1997). Indo-European spread with agriculture or perhaps stockbreeding over a huge area. Sino-Tibetan, Tai-Kadai, and Austronesian spread in Eastern Eurasia with rice farming. The Bantu part of the Niger-Congo lineage spread through much of Africa with the transition to farming. We have no idea how many earlier stocks were overcome by these waves, but there were undoubtedly more than there are

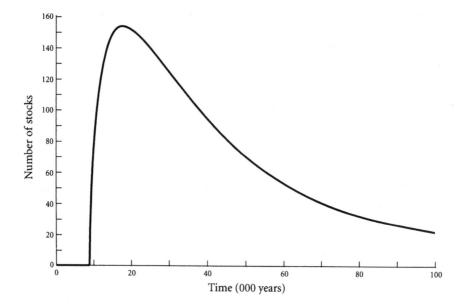

FIGURE 6.2. Predicted number of stocks over time for a notional continent, using the simple model described by equations (1), (2), and (3)

today. The phylogenetic diversity of areas with a clear Neolithic punctuation still appears to us, today, to be low, because there has not been time since the Neolithic for the languages spread by Neolithic transition to become so different that we count them as different stocks.

We can add the effects of a Neolithic punctuation by suddenly increasing the rate of extinction in the continent at a given time associated with the origin of farming, whilst not introducing a rise in the rate of new stocks, since, as we have seen, the Neolithic transition was generally too recent for stocks to have evolved subsequently. Let us assume in our notional continent that a Neolithic transition occurs at 50,000 years after settlement, and that at this point the risk of extinction rises from 5 per cent to 10 per cent per thousand years.

The patterns of stocks over time for continents with and without a Neolithic punctuation of the type described are shown in Figure 6.3. As the figure shows, a Neolithic transition causes a sharp decline in the number of stocks. A reduction of this kind must have followed the spreads of Indo-European, and the other Neolithic lineages with which we are familiar.

This simple model suggest an interpretation of the phylogenetic diversity data displayed in Table 6.1. The high diversity of the Colonized Areas—the Americas,

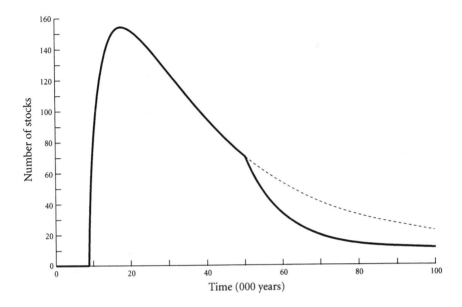

FIGURE 6.3. Predicted number of stocks over time for a notional continent, adding a Neolithic transition 50,000 years after first settlement

Australia, the Pacific—is quite consistent with their more recent habitation than the Old World. Indeed, the particularly high number of stocks of the Americas is indicative not of great age, as Nichols (1990) argues, but of shallow time depth, as Dixon (1997: 94) contends. What we see in the Americas is the profile of a continent soon after the initial radiation of its stocks, before extinction and convergence have reduced their number.[6]

The second factor giving rise to greater diversity in the Colonized Areas is their differences from the Old World in the transition to farming. Both Africa and Eurasia, as we saw in Chapter 5, had early and thorough conversions to farming. This promoted the spread of a few very large stocks that greatly reduced their

---

[6] One of Nichols's (1990: 491) arguments against the plausbility of Greenberg's (1987) proposed Amerind superfamily is that the structure of that lineage involves a very wide—initially six-way—branching structure. This she feels to be unrealistic, arguing that, on the basis of well-established families, we should expect only one or two branches per node. However, I would argue that, following the adaptive radiation reasoning developed here, a wide branching structure is exactly what we should predict when a lineage moves into a new continent with many empty niches. This does not, however, mean that the Amerind proposal should be supported. It is highly dubious for independent methodological reasons (see Campbell 1988; Matisoff 1990; Ringe 1992; McMahon and McMahon 1995).

continents' diversity. Africa and Eurasia are thus on the lower line of Figure 6.3, and a long way along it.

The other continents followed a rather different trajectory. Australia never had a Neolithic transition at all. New Guinea had an early origin of agriculture, but this did not spread to the whole island, and the population boom did not begin until the introduction of the sweet potato thousands of years later. Even then the wave of advance was constrained by New Guinea's unique geography, and agriculture never covered the whole land mass.[7] The Americas had at least three independent agricultural origins, but they were later than those of the Old World, and none of them spread as widely across the continent as the farming complexes did in Eurasia.

These different trajectories are, I would suggest, another reason for the difference of grade apparent in Figure 6.1. The Neolithic spreads have dragged the diversity of the Old World even lower than its great time depth predicts. In the Colonized Areas, Neolithic spreads were limited or absent, and in these areas lineages are not as widespread as in the Old World. They lack any examples of really widespread lineages like Bantu. The closest contender, Polynesian, is the exception that proves the rule, since it originated on the margins of the Old World with a Neolithic transition, and pushed out into the Pacific.

6.6. Validating the Model

The simple numerical model presented here is no more than a heuristic, since I have arbitrarily chosen values for the equations to suit my argument. It serves, none the less, to suggest an interpretation of the facts. In this section I consider whether the general shape of the curve produced by the model can be validated using the data from Table 6.1. If it can, this suggests that the interpretation given above may well be correct.

There are widely available archaeological estimates of the time depth of settlement of the several continents. These are reproduced in Table 6.2. I have adopted the late, Clovis date for the Americas (around 12,000 years ago), though this matter is still subject to controversy. We do not, of course, know how many times the continents were settled independently, and in the absence of such information we have to assume the effect of multiple settlements to be negligible.

The problem in comparing continents is that they differ in size, and so each one requires a different value of A, the constant in the model that reflects the number of available niches. This problem can be solved by calculating the number of stocks in the continent relative to the number of languages, as the number of

---

[7] Agriculture may, however, have been involved in localized lineage spreads in New Guinea, such as that of the Trans New Guinea Phylum (Bellwood 1997: 128–9).

TABLE 6.2. *Approximate time depth of habitation of the major continents and the number of language stocks per thousand languages in them*

Area	Time depth (000 years)	Stocks per 1,000 languages
Africa	>100	7.6
S. and SE Asia	60	5.0
New Guinea	50	24.3
Australia	50	64.1
N. Eurasia	40	24.6
North America	12	208.8
Mesoamerica	12	36.8
South America	12	156.3

languages is some measure of the number of communities that the continent can support. The second column of Table 6.2, then, shows the number of stocks per thousand languages for the major continents (Oceania has been omitted; the numbers are the reciprocals of those in the last column of Table 6.1, multiplied by 1,000).

If the model and interpretation given in the previous section are generally valid, then plotting the stocks per thousand languages measure against time of settlement should give a curve of approximately the shape of Figures 6.2 and 6.3.

Figure 6.4 shows such a plot. If one ignores Mesoamerica, the distribution of points is entirely compatible with the curve of Figure 6.2. Diversity is at a peak in the Americas, and gradually declines to a minimum in the oldest continents. Two anomalies need to be explained: first, Mesoamerica is much lower in diversity than the rest of the Americas, and, secondly, New Guinea is lower in diversity than Australia, though they were settled at the same time. (These statements are relative, of course; the phylogenetic diversity of Australia is only higher than that of New Guinea relative to the number of languages there.)

These discrepancies may well be due to the differences in farming trajectory, as discussed in the previous section. Each of the three American subcontinents had a farming transition. The one in North America spread least far, and the relative diversity is highest in North America. That in South America, based on the potato, spread a little more widely, but the one that was most far-reaching and led to the greatest increase in economic scale was undoubtedly that which took place in Mexico based on maize. This may account for the lowering of relative diversity in Mesoamerica. New Guinea, as we have seen, had some prehistoric agriculture. This may explain why New Guinea's relative diversity is lower than that of Australia, which never had a transition at all.

Overall, then, the data from the main continents conform to the general relationship between stock diversity, time, and farming dispersals that I put

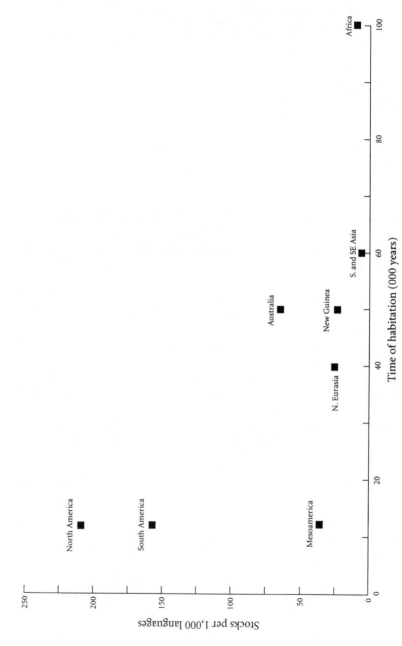

FIGURE 6.4. The number of stocks per thousand languages of the major continents, against their approximate time depth of human habitation

forward in Section 6.5, and show no support at all for the idea that phylogenetic diversity increases linearly with time.

6.7. Conclusions

We have seen in this chapter that phylogenetic diversity, measured at the stock level, is unevenly distributed across the globe, with an order of magnitude more languages per stock in Africa and Eurasia than in America, Australia, or New Guinea. We interpreted this discrepancy, with the aid of a simple heuristic model, as the result of the interaction of great time depth of settlement in Africa and Eurasia with the Neolithic punctuation. If diversity were measured at the level of some shallower unit—the family or subfamily, say—the results might be somewhat different, as there has been sufficient time since the Neolithic for new families to separate. The Old World might thus appear more diverse at this lower level.

Chapters 4, 5, and 6, taken together, show that no simple principle can be formulated for linguistic diversity of the type 'more time, more diversity'. The processes of diversification depend in complex ways on geographical and societal factors, which mean that diversity can increase with time, but can also decrease, or arrive at an equilibrium level. In the remaining chapters of the book we turn to the third type of linguistic diversity mentioned in Chapter 1, structural diversity, with this conclusion in mind.

As a coda to the present chapter, we should consider the likely effect of the ongoing industrial punctuation on phylogenetic diversity in language. We have seen that the transition to farming happened in some language groups and not others, and that, as those farmers then multiplied, their languages were spread with them at the expense of other language families. The same is clearly true of modern economic development, which happened, for whatever reason, only in the populations belonging to a small number of language families. Those families are now spreading rapidly, as more people try to switch into the modern economy and the cultural trappings that go with it. This means that many of the wealth of language stocks discussed in this chapter, stocks that managed to survive through the Neolithic, now face a radically increased danger of extinction. Indo-European, with its English and Spanish daughters, is certainly safe in the long run, as is Sino-Tibetan, which contains Chinese. To these we might add Afroasiatic (Arabic), Austronesian (Bahasa Indonesia), and perhaps Japanese. The future of the other 244 stocks is much less certain.

7 Structural Diversity

7.1. Introduction

In this chapter we turn to the third and final type of diversity in the linguistic pool that was identified in Chapter 1. This is structural diversity. Just as phylogenetic diversity is not necessarily correlated with language diversity, so structural diversity is not necessarily correlated with diversity of the other two types. Lineages of languages that are unrelated can be identical on basic structural parameters, either because of areal convergence, or because of independent evolution to some favoured state. On the other hand, many structural states can exist within what is identifiably a single lineage of languages, since not all parameters are phlyogenetically conservative.

Structural diversity is not a single variable in the way that language diversity and diversity of stocks are. Rather, it is a cover term for many dimensions of variation. There are as many different types of structural diversity as there are identifiable suites of structural items in the grammar of languages. Thus we can talk about diversity in morphological marking, in clause alignment, in constituent order, in syllable structure, and so on. Each of these items can pattern independently; a set of languages can be diverse in morphological typology whilst being homogeneous on constituent order, or vice versa. Linguistic typology is beginning to uncover the correlations between such parameters, and between them and phylogenetic diversity (Dryer 1989, 1991, 1992; Nichols 1992). We also know that some parameters (e.g. Head versus Dependent marking, *sensu* Nichols 1986) are phylogenetically conservative, whilst others (e.g. basic word order, Nichols 1992; Dixon 1997: 21) are labile and prone to diffusion. None the less, it is fair to say that we are still far from any general theory of structural diversity, which would make predictions on such issues as which types of diversity should be found together, and under what circumstances structural diversity should be expected to increase or decrease. We also lack a single index of structural diversity, though it is unclear at present whether this reflects a theoretical gap or an important fact about the topic; if the geographical distributions of diversity on different structural parameters does turn out to be completely independent, then no such index will ever be meaningful.

The treatment of structural diversity in this book will be less thorough than that of language diversity or phylogenetic diversity. The book is, as mentioned in

Chapter 1, primarily a work of linguistic anthropology rather than linguistics proper, and structural diversity takes us far into the heartland of the latter discipline. The explanation of structural diversity is the subject of a large literature in linguistic typology, which cannot be entirely surveyed here. Nor will we provide a general theory of structural diversity of the type referred to above. That would be an undertaking well beyond the scope of the present work. Instead, we will consider briefly how structural diversity might be understood within the general framework that has been put forward so far, and how an anthropological approach might provide additional insights that purely linguistic methodologies could miss. The parameters I have chosen to illustrate my arguments—chiefly word order and the size of phonological inventory—have been chosen for no better reason than that good data are available that illustrate the principles under discussion. No claim is being made that they will turn out to be more important or revealing than other structural items as the study of structural diversity advances.

In Section 7.2, then, we recap on the causes of structural diversity in language. In Section 7.3 we consider how structural diversity is distributed around the world, and consider the relevance of social and geographical factors. These rather general considerations are then illustrated with a case study in Section 7.4, that of diversity in phonological inventories.

7.2. Causes of Structural Diversity

In Chapters 2 and 3 we considered the mechanisms by which diversity in general is produced in language. First, there is variation in speech owing to performance factors and imperfect learning. Secondly, there are amplifiers that fix that variation and turn it into grammatical diversification. The amplifiers are, first, geographical isolation, secondly, social selection, and, thirdly, functional selection. In this section I look again at how these three amplifying mechanisms can combine to produce structural diversity in language. Broadly speaking, geographical isolation and social selection can produce diversity by a process I shall term *linguistic drift*. Functional selection can produce diversity because there are *multiple optima* and *competing motivations* in the space of possible languages. I shall look at each of these processes in turn.

7.2.1. Linguistic drift

Let us recall the neutral model of language change from Chapter 2. This model assumes that learners are biased neither towards nor away from any new linguistic variants that arise in their speech community. The probability of acquiring either a new or an established variant depends simply on that variant's frequency in the speech input. I am not suggesting that the neutral model is correct; it is the simplest possible conceptualization of language change.

Under the neutral model, most new mutations would be expected to die out very quickly, because their initial rarity would lead to learners ignoring them (the so-called averaging and threshold problems of Chapter 2). Thus change is predicted only under rather extreme circumstances (small, very isolated groups, or very high rates of variation), as the computer simulations of Chapter 3 showed. It will be recalled that the addition of social selection made linguistic diversification much more likely. Under social selection, learners prefer to model themselves on the speech of certain highly influential individuals. This mitigates the threshold and averaging problems because much of the linguistic input is ignored in favour of that subset that is typical of high-status role models.

Social selection causes certain variants, which happen to arise in influential high-status speakers, to spread quickly through the population. It must be stressed that the success of these variants has nothing whatever to do with their linguistic properties. They are in no sense superior to their competitors in terms of communicative utility or ease of acquisition. Their success represents an interaction of random variation, chance, and non-linguistic processes. It follows that linguistic changes due to social selection or chance have no overall direction in the space of possible languages. They are akin to what geneticists term *drift*: unpredictable small changes in the gene pool of a species, which do represent not natural selection pushing towards a new optimum, but simply random reshuffling of gene frequencies in a finite population.[1]

At a microscopic level, much linguistic change must be seen as drift in this sense. Small changes in the realization of sounds, or in the environment of phonological processes, seem to have no communicative implications, and their success must simply be due to the chance falling-out of social factors and random variation. However, drift cannot be the sole modality of linguistic evolution. If it were, different changes within a language would be completely uncoordinated, and over time languages could be expected to range around arbitrarily over the space of possible grammars. We know that this is not what happens.

Instead, there are relations of co-implication amongst many logically independent linguistic items, which means the presence of one in a language changes the probability of presence of the others in that same language. Such relationships have been identified in many domains of linguistic structure, and some have been mentioned in earlier chapters. Phonological examples will be discussed in Section 7.4. Here we consider just the example of word order.

The order in which a language places the object and verb of a sentence is

---

[1] This usage of the term *drift*, which I shall be adopting, is quite different from that implied in Sapir's (1921/1970) discussion of 'drift' in language change. He meant sustained, directional change in the history of a language, whereas I mean essentially random fluctuations in the frequency of variants.

logically distinct from the order in which it places a noun and a relative clause. However, across the world's languages, these two items are correlated, even when the confounding effects of common ancestry are taken into account (Greenberg 1966; Hawkins 1983; Dryer 1992). Languages with OV order tend to place relative clauses, adpositional phrases, and genitives before the noun, and to use post-positions rather than prepositions, with significantly greater frequency than languages with VO order. Thus the presence of one item alters the probability of presence (or persistence) of the other items in the suite.

In Chapters 2 and 3 such interactions were considered as a type of functional selection. The presence of item A biases language users towards the acquisition or use of items B and C. This can happen in two ways. First, some processing strategy required by item A may incidentally make items B and C easier to process than their alternatives. In the word-order case, for example, the presence of OV order in sentences requires the language user to adopt an appropriate parsing strategy, a parsing strategy that then makes adpositional phrases with the adposition last easier to parse than ones in which the adposition is initial (Hawkins 1983). This is because of a general *harmony* between OV order and Noun–Postposition order; they both place the phrasal category last within the phrase.[2]

The second way in which one item may make the presence of another more likely is through what Croft (1990: 197) calls a 'conspiracy'. This is where the form one item takes creates a functional need for another item. For example, in many languages, the formation of relative clauses is allowed only where the relativized noun (or its trace) will be the subject of the relative clause, not the object or any other constituent. However, real communicative situations often demand that a relative clause be formed of which the relativized noun is not the subject. Languages that allow only subject relatives, then, tend to evolve grammatical processes like the English passive, which allow a non-subject noun to be promoted to subject. Once promoted, it can form the basis of a relative clause. Thus the form the relativization-rule item takes creates a niche for a promotion-to-subject item, which the demands of language use then select for.

As we saw in Section 2.4.2, the difficulty with invoking functional considerations to explain patterns of structural diversity was that functional selection seems likely to lead to uniformity. Human beings, their cognitive and articulatory apparatus, are the same everywhere. We might, therefore, expect every language to evolve towards the same optimal combination of parameters, and then stay there.

In fact, there are strong statistical tendencies for languages to prefer one variant over another in many domains. Around 96 per cent of all languages have subject before object, and around 86 per cent have subject before verb. These

---

[2] The theory of cross-category harmony was developed by Hawkins (1983); the details of the principle have been challenged and amended by Dryer (1992), but the spirit of Dryer's alternative 'Branching Direction Theory' is, for present purposes, fairly similar.

patterns probably reflect universal functional biases—towards having heavier constituents after lighter ones, for example, and towards a flow of information that reflects the cause–effect relationships in the world iconically (see Croft 1990 for a discussion).

Preferences of this kind, then, reflect the effects of functional selection as described in Chapter 2. The question that remains is why there are any languages at all that depart from the preferred pattern. Where the statistical preference is very strong, as in the subject before object case, the rare languages that do depart from the norm are probably just instances of drift. In this case, one would expect them to return to the dominant order fairly soon. This claim has some potentially interesting consequences; one is the prediction that the probability of drifting away from the optimum position will be greater in small communities. This idea will be considered in Section 7.3.

Where the statistical preference is less strong, and especially where the rarer variant can be shown to be diachronically or areally stable, it is likely that some force other than mere drift is at work, and this force is most likely to be a competing functional motivation.

7.2.2. Multiple optima and competing motivations

Linguistic items come under selection in the acquisition and use of language for many different reasons. These include, at the very least, their parsability, economy, iconicity, memory load, and discriminability (Croft 1990: ch. 7). Many of these functional motivations conflict, and, in the complex landscape defined by them, it is likely that there are many local optima into which languages may settle.

To give an example, the most common word-order configuration, once statistical accidents are accounted for, is to have the order SOV, with which the use of postpositions and the order Relative Clause–Noun are generally associated. However, there is a very large number of languages, particularly in Eurasia and Africa, which show instead SOV order, prepositions, and the order Noun–Relative Clause. There is no evidence of a global historical trend towards one pattern or the other.[3] Rather, we must assume that there is a local optimum at SVO, with the other parameters in harmony with it, whence there is no general advantage to mutations taking the language in the direction of SOV and the opposite adposition and relative-clause orders. Languages might sometimes make the transition, none the less, but this will be due to the interaction of drift and function, as I shall discuss in the next section. Thus no one language type is absolutely optimal; rather there are combinations of items that form relatively stable, locally optimal sets. I shall illustrate the ideas of competing motivations and multiple optima more fully in the phonological case study of Section 7.4.

---

[3] Indeed Tomlin's (1986) proposed explanations for word-order frequencies in terms of cognitive and communicative factors rate SOV and SVO as equally optimal.

7.2.3. Interaction of function and drift

What are the relative contributions of functional selection and drift in the evolution of languages? This question is difficult to answer in the abstract. It seems likely that at the microscopic level there is a very high rate of drift, owing to the great importance of social selection. Usually, however, drift moves languages only short distances in the state space; minor sound changes, regularization or acquisition of irregular forms, and so on. Larger departures from a stable language type will come under what biologists know as stabilizing selection, the force that keeps the mean of biological distributions in the same place for long periods.

Occasionally, however, the effects of drift may happen to push a language across to the alternative variant on some far-reaching item such as VO order. Such a change would then affect the functional selection acting on many other items, because of the processing harmony and conspiracy principles identified in the previous section. The language would then undergo a rapid reorganization on many parameters until it conformed to the opposite stable type. Drift, then, pushes languages around within the basin of attraction of a stable typological configuration, and from time to time it may push them over the edge of the basin, whence they tumble rapidly into the bottom of the next basin. The occasional transitions between SVO and SOV order can be interpreted in this way (see Croft 1990: ch. 8[4]).

7.3. Geographical Distribution of Structural Diversity

We have discussed the mechanisms that give rise to structural diversity in language. The next questions concern how structural diversity is distributed in the languages of the world and why. Is there any global patterning of structural diversity, as there was for language diversity and phylogenetic diversity?

7.3.1. Structural diversity across continents

The clearest generalization we can make about structural diversity is that every item seems to pattern differently. Nichols's (1992) survey of a controlled sample of the world's languages gives good examples of this. Nichols plots the global distribution of a large set of grammatical items, and finds that the frequency of

---

[4] Note, though, that the situation as discussed by Croft is more complex than this. Many items may be much more likely to drift in one direction than another because variation is not random but directed. None the less languages do not all converge on the same state, since, for example, the order of verb and object might tend to drift one way, dragging the order of noun and relative clause after it because of the harmony principle, whilst the order of noun and relative clause might inherently tend to drift the other way, dragging the order of verb and object behind it, resulting in an unstable and ceaseless oscillation.

TABLE 7.1. *Data on structural diversity for the nine continental and subcontinental areas of the world*

Area	Language density	Languages per stock	Head-marking uniformity	Alignment uniformity	Complexity uniformity	Word-order uniformity
Africa	88.8	130.7	63	100	42	47
N. Eurasia	21.5	40.7	57	72	53	62
S. and SE Asia	110.4	199.8	80	60	50	50
Oceania	322.1	76.5	57	57	57	40
New Guinea	1197.6	41.1	37	79	67	93
Australia	30.4	15.6	53	42	47	47
North America	12.3	4.9	61	68	68	56
Mesoamerica	144.2	27.2	80	50	50	62
South America	33.3	6.4	54	64	77	60

Source: Nichols 1992, except for language density and languages per stock, which are from Table 6.1.

these items is very variable from continent to continent, and also that the areas that are most diverse on one item are the least diverse on others. Table 7.1 abstracts some key patterns from her data. It concerns four key grammatical items identified in Nichols's survey. They are:

1. the dominant locus of morphological marking (on the head of the phrase, or on its dependents);
2. the alignment of the clause (nominative–accusative, like English, ergative, or stative–active);
3. the degree of morphological complexity (high, medium, or low);
4. the basic word order (verb initial, verb medial, or verb final).

The linguistic details of these items are well discussed by Nichols herself (1992: ch. 2); what concerns us here is the geographical distribution of diversity.

Continents differ with regard to which variant of the four items is most common. Verb finality is the dominant order in most areas, for example, but verb mediality is more common in Australia, and verb initiality is more common in Mesoamerica. Nichols ascertains which is the most common variant of each item in each geographical area. She then calculates the frequency of occurrence of that modal variant in all the languages she samples from that area. This frequency, expressed as a percentage, gives an index of the internal uniformity of the area on the item in question. A value of 100 per cent means that all sample languages from the area are the same, whilst a lower value means more diversity.

Table 7.1 shows the uniformity percentages for the four items for the nine geographical areas used in Chapter 5. It is clear that areas that are highly diverse on one item are quite uniform on another. Africa, for example, is completely uniform on clause alignment, but highly diverse in word order and morphological complexity. Overall, there are no significant correlations between uniformity on one item and uniformity on the others (Spearman rank correlations; $n = 9$, n.s.).

Table 7.1 also shows the language-density and languages-per-stock figures from Chapter 6. These give rough measures of language diversity and phylogenetic diversity for the different areas. Once again, there is no correlation between those types of diversity and the uniformity of the structural items (Spearman rank correlations; $n = 9$, n.s.).

Structural diversity, at least on the items shown here, thus shows no overall pattern and no correlation with other types of diversity. The most likely explanation for this is that each item propagates itself well under different circumstances. Clause alignment, for example, is thought to be phylogenetically conservative (Nichols 1992: 167). This means that it will tend to be more diverse where there are many independent lineages of languages evolving, and diversity in alignment is indeed great in New Guinea and the Americas, and low in Africa, where the number of stocks is relatively low. Word order, on the other hand, is extremely prone to areal convergence. The chief vector for this appears to be bilingualism.

The processing and parsing habits of the bilingual brain lead to the word order of one language interfering with that of another wherever there is a substantial number of people speaking both languages. (This is just an extension of the harmony argument about word-order patterns discussed in Section 7.2.) Now, where the density of different languages is very high, as in New Guinea, it may be common for people to be fluent in several of them. This provides a vector for word-order convergence, and indeed New Guinea, with its huge number of languages, is actually rather uniform with respect to word order.

Thus each item spreads in different ways and will support diversity under different societal and geographical circumstances, a fact that probably accounts for the lack of correlations in Table 7.1, and the chaotic mosaic obtained by plotting the geography of different structural items.

7.3.2. Drift and the sociolinguistic setting

We have seen that the force of drift pushes languages around in the space of possible grammars, with functional considerations dictating the location of the optima where they can settle. This picture raises a further question: what is it that determines which languages end up in which optima? It might simply be a chance-driven, random walk process, so that every language had in principle the same probability of ending up at a given point in the state space.

The alternative possibility, which was raised briefly in Section 2.4.2, is that certain non-linguistic contexts favour the persistence of certain items. This is clearly true at a lexical level; words for sand, ice, and fish species, for example, are unevenly distributed amongst languages in proportion to the importance those domains have for different peoples (though the claim that Eskimos have dozens of words for snow is largely apocryphal (see Pullum 1991)). Whether there are any relationships between language evolution and the societal context at the level of grammar is more uncertain. Kaye (1989: 48), who was quoted in Section 2.4.2, is in accord with most contemporary linguists when he says that no such inter-actions exist.

Kaye's claim, however, is not backed up with any empirical evidence. Whilst it remains true that no relationships of grammatical typology to culture or social organization have been convincingly demonstrated (with the marginal exception of Perkins 1992), the general absence of a relationship has not been demonstrated either. In fact, the question has received little rigorous scholarly attention. In the framework outlined here, it seems quite plausible that some such relationship could exist. Certain types of social network or communicative situation could well select for one variant item over another.

Any successful argument that the sociolinguistic setting affects the evolution of grammar would have to do two things. First, it would need to demonstrate a statistically valid cross-linguistic, cross-cultural correlation between a linguistic parameter and some non-linguistic situation. Secondly, it would need to provide a plausible mechanism whereby the non-linguistic trait had influenced the evolution of the linguistic one. Such a project is well beyond the scope of this book, and is not attempted here. This is an avenue that future research on linguistic diversity might pursue. However, by way of stimulating discussion, in this and the next section I will consider the possible effect of one societal variable on language change. That variable is community size. In this section I will draw on the example of word order to illustrate the argument.

As we have seen, word orders in which subject precedes object are overwhelmingly common in the world's languages. There are, however, a few cases of each of the word orders that do not conform to this patterns—VOS, OVS, and OSV. The object-inital orders are particularly rare, and they were not even considered possible until a few decades ago (see Pullum 1981 for a catalogue of languages with these word orders).

As I have already argued, the tendency for subject to precede object is probably the result of some functional principle of language use that biases language evolution, of the kind proposed by Tomlin (1986). The minor orders probably represent non-optimal positions into which drift may none the less push languages from time to time. One would predict that they will not stay there indefinitely, but would return to the favoured state in due course.[5]

In population genetics, it is well known that the effects of random drift are greater when the population is small. This is because the probability of a slightly deleterious variant becoming fixed in a population is inversely related to the population size (Kimura 1983). The smaller the community, the greater the stochastic effects of chance changes in gene frequency.

I have argued elsewhere that a similar principle might apply to linguistic communities (Nettle, forthcoming *b*). Drift occurs because of the random conjunction of variation, learning, and social influence that happens in finite, structured populations. If a group consists of just a few hundred people, the idiosyncracies of one very influential individual can spread through it very easily. This is not the case if the group consists of thousands or tens of thousands of people. In general, the smaller the community, the greater the probability that a given variant that has no functional advantage at all, but is neutral or slightly disadvantageous, can replace the existing item and become the norm. Computer simulations in Nettle (forthcoming *b*) bear this conclusion out.

If the foregoing arguments are correct, one could predict that the rare, non-optimal orders would be more likely to be found in small communities than in large ones, since these would be more vulnerable to drift away from optimal states. This is a difficult hypothesis to test. By amalgamating reports from several

---

[5] Though see Pullum (1982) for the argument that there may be no linguistic bias against the rarer word orders, and that their scarcity is just historical accident. This argument seems to me implausible.

sources in the literature (Pullum 1981; Tomlin 1986; Nichols 1992), I have found nineteen claimed cases of object-initial orders. These are listed in Table 7.2 along with the number of their speakers where this is available. For the Australian languages, I have used the calculation made in Chapter 4 that the average group size was around 3,000 individuals.

TABLE 7.2. *Languages with object-initial word orders*

Language	Location	Speakers
Apalaí	Brazil	150
Apurinā	Brazil	1,000
Arecuna	Brazil	?
Asuriní	Brazil	50
Bacairí	Brazil	250
Barasano	Colombia	?
Fasu	New Guinea	1,200
Hanis	USA	extinct
Hianacoto	Colombia	?
Hixkaryana	Brazil	350
Hurrian	Near East	extinct
Jamamadi	Brazil	180
Macushi	Venezuela	16,000
Mangarayi	Australia	3,000[a]
Nadëb	Brazil	150
Panare	Venezuela	1,000
Ungarinjin	Australia	3000[a]
Urubú	Brazil	500
Xavante	Brazil	3,000

[a] inferred figure.

Sources: Pullum 1981; Tomlin 1986; Nichols 1992.

The median size of the communities in Table 7.2 is 750. The median number of speakers for a human language in general is much greater: 5,000, using the SIL database. Thus of the fourteen object-initial languages for which there are data, only one (Macushi) is larger than the median size of a language in general, whilst thirteen are smaller. It does thus seem that there is an association between object-initial order and community size.

Great care must be taken with data such as these, however, since the languages involved may not be phylogenetically or areally independent. If we count each one as a separate evolution of object-initiality, we will certainly overestimate any association of group size and word order. At worst, it may turn out that there are only five independent instances of object-initial orders evolving; one in tropical

South America, one in the United States, one in the ancient Near East, one in New Guinea, and one in Australia. Of these, we have no community size information for the US case or the ancient Near-Eastern one; but, in the other three cases, we can say with confidence that it arose in very small groups.

Thus it seems that the aberrant, object-initial word orders may indeed be more likely to be found in small communities. The case presented here that community size is important requires further investigation, but it does suggest one way in which the non-linguistic setting could influence the interplay of drift and function in linguistic evolution. Many others could also be conceived of. In the next section I revisit all the themes of this chapter with an empirical case study—that of the evolution of diversity in phonological structure.

7.4. Case Study: Phonological Inventory and the Lexicon

An important breakthrough in the scientific study of language was the realization that each language used only a finite and determinate number of contrastive sounds. It was also immediately clear that the inventory of these sounds differed very considerably from language to language. This variation, however, is not unconstrained. First, all languages basically employ vowels as the nuclei of words and syllables, flanked with varying numbers of consonants. Secondly, there are hierarchies of preference as to which sounds are favoured. Cross-language surveys show that, if a language has three vowels, they will be [i a u]; if five, they will usually be [i e a o u], and so on for inventories of different sizes (Maddieson 1984). Similarly, consonants of simple articulation such as [p t k] are found in small phonological inventories, with more complex articulations occurring in larger inventories only once the basic options are used up (Lindblom and Maddieson 1988). In short, given the information that a phonological inventory contains a certain number of vowels and a certain number of consonants, one can predict reasonably closely what those vowels and consonants will be.

The theory of functional selection offers explanations for these patterns. Let us take the vowel and consonant cases separately.

Individual vowel segments move around the phonetic space by drift, as we have seen in Chapter 3. Given that each sound is a separate item, it is perhaps surprising that there appears to be coordination between them, until we realize that the coordination is an emergent property of the interactions between the items. If two vowel segments drift too close together, then one of two things will happen. Learners of the language may fail to discriminate the two sound classes, and acquire a version of the language in which the distinction has been lost altogether, as happens in the frequent cases of 'phoneme merger'. Alternatively, since sound tokens in speech are widely scattered around the phonetic centre for the type, learners may misinterpret some of the tokens of segment A as tokens of segment

B. Their model of what constitutes segment A will then be skewed away from the phonetic vicinity of B, and this will be reflected in their speech production. If this process is iterated, A and B will continue to move apart until they are maximally distant from each other in the available phonetic space. The optima for this evolutionary process are combinations of sounds that minimize the probability of tokens of any one vowel being confused with tokens of another. Lindblom (1986) has shown that the patterns we typically observe in natural language—[i a u] for example—tend to be such optima, thus providing a neat theoretical explanation for the cross-linguistic patterns.

In the consonant case, the functional principle that ensures that languages evolve towards the simplest inventory of consonants probably involves under-articulation. We know that speakers will under-articulate tokens to the extent that the communicative situation allows them to (Lieberman 1963). For example, the implosives [ɓ] and [ɗ] may be produced as plain [b] and [d] in many instances in real speech. We assume that the speaker tends to avoid potential communicative failure, and so will make the implosive/plain distinction clearly where the interpretation of meaning depends upon it.[6] However, where no meaning hangs on the distinction, as in a hypothetical language which has /ɓ/ and /ɗ/ but not /b/ and /d/, the speaker may without cost make the reduction all the time. When this becomes common, future learners of the language are likely to acquire the plain consonants for what used to be the implosives, with the latter quickly disappearing from the language. This would seem to explain the finding that no language has /ɓ/ and /ɗ/ that does not already have /b/ and /d/. For most complex consonants, there is a plain equivalent for which such a statement holds true, and the tendency to under-articulate where the situation permits would seem to provide a quite general explanation.

Given that the combination of segments a language employs is to some extent predictable, most of the variation between languages in sound structure resides on two dimensions. The first is the total size of the inventory. The second is the ratio of vowels to consonants. In the following sections, I deal with the first of these dimensions. In Section 7.4.1 I put forward a competing motivations theory of how phonological inventories evolve to different sizes, which I then test in Section 7.4.2.

7.4.1. Inventory size and word length: Competing motivations

In calculations using the traditional definition of the phoneme, the number of segments used by different languages is extremely variable—from a minimum of

---

[6] Labov (1994: ch. 19) discusses a number of cases where there is evidence that speakers do not choose the variant that preserves meaning distinctions. These are clearly problematic for accounts of sound change based on functional selection. For the present argument, however, all that is required is that the preservation of meaning has *some influence* on which variants persist; it need not be the only or largest influence.

eleven to perhaps 141 (Maddieson 1984). Elsewehere I have used a slightly different definition of the segment (Nettle 1995). In tone languages, I count each permitted combination of vowel and tone separately, since each one represents a permitted and contrastive possibility for one phonological position. Thus, for a language with five vowels and four contrastive tones, I calculate twenty possible vowel segments.

Using this definition, the smallest inventories in the world are still around eleven segments, but the largest are much larger: 195 for the Niger-Congo language Vute (Guarisma 1988), for example. We should thus ask what the mechanisms are that cause inventories to grow and shrink in size.

Languages gain phonological segments through a combination of coarticulation and word truncation. Coarticulation is the tendency for successive sounds to alter each other phonetically in the stream of speech. Thus a vowel that follows a nasal consonant, for example, will take on some nasal phonetic characteristics. Truncation of word forms occurs in speech performance (Lieberman 1963), and this widespread tendency means that learners may acquire a shorter underlying form than that of their parents, and so words often shorten in the history of languages (Lüdtke 1986). Where words become truncated, contrast is maintained by hearers using the colouring left on earlier parts of the word by the now-deleted material as a cue. Word-final nasal consonants in French, for example, have disappeared, but the vowels that used to precede them have become nasal vowels. Presumably, this evolved gradually as speakers transferred the nasal cues to the vowel and could thus clip off the consonantal articulation without so much loss of contrast. Eventually, new generations of learners reanalysed the system as having a set of nasal vowels and shorter words with no final consonants. A similar process has often been observed in tone languages (Hombert 1972; Matisoff 1973). Contrasts in voicing on syllable-final consonants are gradually transferred to contrasts in pitch on the preceding vowel. The consonants may then disappear, leaving shorter words and an extra set of phonological contrasts—namely, high and low tone. In general, then, the forces of articulatory economy in the history of a language lead to the truncation of individual words, and a concomitant increase in the number of contrastive segments.

Inventories do not, however, keep growing forever. There must be forces that reduce or stabilize the number of segments working in opposition to those that increase it. The incorporation of extra vowels or consonants into the inventory reduces the acoustic and perceptual distance between them.[7] The larger the inventory, the more crowded the perceptual space will be.

[7] This also applies to tones. Tones exist in a finite acoustic space, and must be distinguishable from each other (Hombert 1972). Laboratory studies of tone perception suggest that the maximum number of tone levels that can be reliably distinguished is five (Pollack 1952). Few languages use the possible range; though five levels have been observed (Longacre 1952), four levels or fewer are much more common.

As the inventory gets larger, and the segments more crowded together, we might therefore expect an increase in the probability of listeners failing to discriminate adjacent segments from each other. If learners cannot reliably distinguish two segments, they will not make the distinction in their own production, and it may disappear from the language, thus reducing the size of the inventory. This is a segment merger; as a result, sets of words that were previously distinct become homophones.

When words have become homophones, speakers may have to compensate by some kind of lexical strategy, such as coining a new word or paraphrase. In Chinese, for example, a series of phonological mergers led to a large class of previously distinct monosyllables becoming homophones. In many of these cases, one of the pair of homophones has now been replaced by an unambiguous bisyllabic compound. Thus the morphological expansion compensates for the loss of phonological contrast.

Discrimination failure leads to smaller inventories, and the lexical strategies by which meaning is maintained tend to produce longer word forms. The pressure on the language from discrimination failure thus precisely balances that due to articulatory economy. The actual system of any given language emerges from a dynamic equilibrium between these two factors. Differences in inventory size are the result of different balances between articulatory and perceptual pressures.

If this competing-motivations account is correct, there should be a trade-off between word length and inventory size: the larger the phonological inventory of a language, the shorter its words should be. In the next section I will test whether this prediction holds good for a sample of unrelated languages.

7.4.2. Testing the theory

The methods used for testing the hypothesized trade-off between the size of the phonological inventory of a language and the word length are described in full in Nettle (1995) and Nettle (1998c). Those papers tested it on two different samples of languages; ten languages from all over the world in Nettle (1995), and twelve languages from West Africa in Nettle (1998c). For the present illustration, a composite sample of ten languages has been produced from among the twenty-two in the two earlier papers. All ten of these belong to different language families, and they are widely dispersed geographically. The sample has no pretence at coverage of all the world's regions or language stocks, but the languages in question are at least completely independent of each other.

For each language, the average length of an uninflected word form is determined by taking a random sample of fifty stems from a sizeable dictionary. The size of the phonological inventory is ascertained from a good phonological description, following the principle I have outlined above, by which each combination of vowel and tone for tone languages is counted separately.

TABLE 7.3. *The size of the phonological inventory (S) and the mean word length (L) for ten languages*

Language	Segmental inventory size	Mean word length
Georgian	34	7.74
Hausa	35	5.68
Hawaiian	36	5.26
Italian	30	7
!Kung	147	4.02
Mandarin	53	5.4
Tamasheq	36	5.26
Thai	76	3.65
Turkish	28	6.44
Vute	195	3.94

Sources: Nettle (1995, 1998c).

The data, abstracted from Nettle (1995) and Nettle (1998c), are presented in Table 7.3. According to the hypothesis, there should be an inverse relationship between the size of phonological inventory (S) and the mean word length (L). Figure 7.1 shows that this is indeed the case. The relationship is modelled by the equation:

$$L = 17.54 \ S^{-0.30}$$
$$(r = 0.86, \ d.f. = 8, \ p < 0.05)$$

The prediction of the competing-motivations account is thus met. Average word length is inversely related to the size of the phonological inventory, and we can see the balance between the two as some kind of equilibrium between forces of economy that tend to truncate words and multiply phonological distinctions, and perceptual constraints that cause distinctions to be lost and words to be made longer.

We might reasonably ask why different languages find such different balances between the two forces. Why should the Khoisan !Kung, with its clicks and rich tonal system, end up with such an extremely large inventory, whilst Hawaiian has moved to the other extreme? This may simply be the result of drift, which moves languages randomly up and down on both dimensions, but never taking them too far from the optimal trade-off curve. Alternatively, there could once again be an interaction with population size. We might assume that the optimum value for L and S is somewhere in the middle of the distribution. Drift can, however, pull languages off toward the extremes. If, as I suggested in the previous section, drift has more extreme effects in smaller populations, then the languages of small

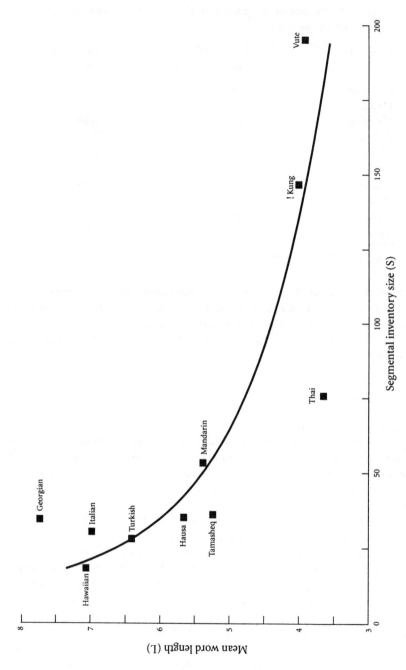

FIGURE 7.1. The size of the phonological inventory (S) against the mean word length (L) for ten languages

communities would be much more likely to venture into the extremes of the distribution than those of larger ones.

Anecdotally, this prediction seems plausible, and there is some support for it from African languages (Nettle 1998c). The largest inventories I have documented belong to !Kung, spoken by a few thousand hunter-gatherers in the Kalahari, and Vute and some related languages spoken by small groups of farmers along the Nigeria–Cameroon border. More widespread African languages in the sample have smaller inventories. Elsewhere, very small inventories are typical of Australia, New Guinea, and the Pacific, where community size is generally very small. There is no instance to my knowledge of a language spoken by millions of people with either an extremely large or an extremely small inventory of sounds. This is, however, somewhat speculative. An attempt to test this hypothesis statistically using a global sample of languages found no general support for it (Nettle 1996a). Furthermore, very small inventories are an extremely stable areal characteristic of the Australo-Pacific region, which is hardly what one would expect if they are produced by drift and are generally selected against.

The results of this case study, then, are only partially satisfying. We can give a good account of how languages come to have different-sized phonological inventories in terms of different trade-offs between economy and discriminability. Why different languages find the different equilibria that they do is another question that demands much further investigation, and might perhaps reflect nothing more than the action of chance.

7.5. Conclusions

The account of sound structure put forward here is just one example of how cross-linguistic patterns can be explained using a model that assumes that (combinations of) linguistic items come under functional selection by speakers and learners in the history of languages. The same logic can be applied to many further issues in phonology,[8] as well as to many other areas of linguistic structure, and indeed this is being done within the burgeoning functional–typological paradigm within linguistics (e.g. Hawkins 1983, 1994; Tomlin 1986; Croft 1990; Bybee *et al.* 1994; Kirby 1999).

As this research continues, the question will continue to arise as to why some communities have found certain structural equilibria in the space of possible languages, whilst others have found quite different ones. The answer may be that their trajectories reflect nothing more than the action of random drift. However, it also seems quite possible that it will transpire that non-linguistic factors are relevant. Community size is one that I have discussed; other more difficult ones

---

[8] Note that I have not dealt with the issue of the vowel/consonant ratio, nor others such as the evolution of syllable structure constraints, which vary considerably from language to language.

to quantify include the openness of communities to outsiders and foreigners, the fluidity of social groups, the prevalence of exogamy, and the structure of individuals' social networks. I hope that this is an area where linguistic anthropology, in a properly pluralistic framework, may contribute to the development of linguistics proper.

Epilogue

No epilogue, I pray you; for your play needs no excuse.
(*A Midsummer Night's Dream*)

Summary

We have now reached the end of our enquiry into linguistic diversity. The mechanisms that produce it were considered, and three different levels of diversity were identified (Section 1.3). Each of these levels was then examined in turn.

Linguistic items change by a process of descent with modification. This process was considered in Chapters 2 and 3. The sources of variation in language are speech performance and imperfect learning. These alone cannot account for linguistic diversification, since they tend to be averaged out in the process of language acquisition. Variation is, however, amplified by geographical isolation, social selection, and functional selection in such a way that, given enough time, completely different languages can evolve. Computer simulations suggest that social selection is fundamental to the origin and maintenance of linguistic diversity, and I have suggested that social selection takes place because of the important role language has in the distinctive marking of social groups.

The first type of linguistic diversity discussed was variation in the number of languages, or *language diversity* (Chapters 4 and 5). The factors influencing its distribution were investigated. In subsistence economies, the most important is the ecological regime in which the people live. Seasonal climates produce large ethnolinguistic groups because people form large networks of exchange to mitigate the subsistence risk to which they are exposed. Non-seasonal, equatorial climates such as those of Papua New Guinea and Zaire produce numerous small ethnolinguistic groups, as reliable self-sufficiency in basic subsistence is achievable.

This pattern dates from the Neolithic, and is now being upset by the development of the modern economy, which pulls or drags people into much wider social networks. Many or most small languages are in danger of disappearing as the spread and growth of the modern economy continues.

The second type of diversity to be considered was *phylogenetic diversity* (Chapter 6), which is variation in the number of lineages of languages. It was argued that phylogenetic diversity tends to be at its height a few thousand years after the radiation of peoples that typically follows the first settlement of a continent. The Americas are an example of a continent in this state. Thereafter, phylogenetic diversity declines owing to lineage extinction, leading to an eventual dominance of a few huge lineages, often spread by farming, such as one sees in Africa.

The final type of diversity was structural (Chapter 7). Languages come to vary in their structure on any dimension along which there is variation in production and acquisition. Sometimes that diversity represents simple random drift around optimal language systems. In other cases, different systems represent different, locally optimal solutions to the same problems, or different trade-offs between competing motivations. The question of why languages in some regions follow certain paths while those elsewhere follow others deserves further investigation.

I believe that some light has been shed on the patterns and processes underlying diversity in human language at all three of our levels, though the findings presented here are far from exhaustive. The questions posed have been of a very general nature, and the analysis has involved a great deal of simplification of the facts and the factors involved. Simplification is not necessarily falsification, though, and I hope that the detailed quantitative tests I have applied to my hypotheses where possible provide adequate justification for my claims. None the less, the broad trends outlined here need to be connected to more focused empirical studies to understand the patterns in more detail and to subject our explanations for them to more rigorous scrutiny. When these issues are more firmly understood, we can pursue on a firmer basis the exciting task of relating linguistic diversity to human diversity of other kinds; genetic, archaeological, and cultural.

Envoi

The objective of this book has been to elucidate the patterns of diversity we see in human language, and the processes that caused those patterns to evolve. Normal disciplinary boundaries were set aside in order to give a holistic treatment of phenomena that proved complex and multifaceted. I feel that this holism was justified because a number of significant and interesting patterns were observed. These would never have been visible from the partial perspective of any one disciplinary tradition.

I argued that the ethnolinguistic map is a product of people's social behaviour, and that social behaviour is motivated by the economic necessities of subsistence. The subsistence economy is in turn linked to the ecological setting. In short, I have dealt with various domains of facts—linguistic, sociocultural, economic, and ecological—and concluded that, rather than being entirely autonomous, they can influence each other. Human history does not take place in a series of watertight compartments. It is a manifold of interlocking causal chains, with the human individual at its centre.

It took chemists hundreds of years to realize that, behind all the facts about metals, facts about liquids, facts about gases, and so on, there was a single explanatory factor: the behaviour of subatomic particles in different circumstances. Similarly, there are linguistic facts, geographical facts, cultural facts, economic facts, and so on. Ultimately, however, I feel that these should all be explained in terms of individual human beings, their natures, and their behaviour in the different situations in which they find themselves. This is the promise of a unified anthropology, a promise we have tried to live up to here.

The paraphrase from William Labov with which this endeavour was introduced (Section 1.6) ran:

> a set of propositions that relate general findings about linguistic diversity to general properties of human beings or of human societies will deserve to be called a theory of linguistic diversity. (after Labov 1994: 5)

We may not yet have achieved such a theory, but I hope we have made some road towards one.

APPENDIX

Global Language Diversity Data

This appendix contains the data on global linguistic diversity discussed in Chapter 4. The countries are listed alphabetically.

Country	Langs	Area	Pop.	Stations	MGS	Std
Algeria	18	2,381,741	25,660	102	6.60	2.29
Angola	42	1,246,700	10,303	50	6.22	1.87
Australia	234	7,713,364	17,336	134	6.00	4.17
Bangladesh	37	143,998	118,745	20	7.40	0.73
Benin	52	112,622	4,889	7	7.14	0.99
Bolivia	38	1,098,581	7,612	48	6.92	2.50
Botswana	27	581,730	1,348	10	4.60	1.69
Brazil	209	8,511,965	153,322	245	9.71	5.87
Burkina Faso	75	274,000	9,242	6	5.17	1.07
CAR	94	622,984	3,127	13	8.08	1.21
Cambodia	18	181,035	8,442	9	8.44	0.50
Cameroon	275	475,422	12,239	35	9.17	1.75
Chad	126	1,284,000	5,819	11	4.00	1.81
Colombia	79	1,138,914	33,613	35	11.37	1.37
Congo	60	342,000	2,346	10	9.60	1.69
Costa Rica	10	51,100	3,064	38	8.92	1.78
Côte d'Ivoire	75	322,463	12,464	9	8.67	1.25
Cuba	1	110,861	10,736	13	7.46	1.55
Ecuador	22	283,561	10,851	44	8.14	3.47
Egypt	11	1,001,449	54,688	50	0.89	0.89
Ethiopia	112	1,221,900	53,383	36	7.28	3.10
French Guiana	11	90,000	102	5	10.40	0.80
Gabon	40	267,667	1,212	14	8.79	0.77
Ghana	73	238,553	15,509	28	8.79	1.68
Guatemala	52	108,889	9,467	59	9.31	2.23
Guinea	29	245,857	5,931	8	7.38	1.22
Guyana	14	214,969	800	5	12.00	0.00
Honduras	9	112,088	5,265	13	8.54	2.53
India	405	3,287,590	849,638	218	5.32	1.92
Indonesia	701	1,904,569	187,765	58	10.67	1.82

Country	Langs	Area	Pop.	Stations	MGS	Std
Kenya	58	580,367	25,905	34	7.26	3.61
Laos	93	236,800	4,262	7	7.14	0.35
Liberia	34	111,369	2,705	21	10.62	0.84
Libya	13	1,759,540	4,712	54	2.43	1.60
Madagascar	4	587,041	11,493	81	7.33	2.96
Malawi	14	118,484	8,556	20	5.80	1.50
Malaysia	140	329,749	18,333	63	11.92	0.37
Mali	31	1,240,192	9,507	17	3.59	1.97
Mauritania	8	1,025,520	2,036	8	0.75	0.83
Mexico	243	1,958,201	87,836	272	5.84	2.69
Mozambique	36	801,590	16,084	90	6.07	1.39
Myanmar	105	676,578	42,561	30	6.93	0.81
Namibia	21	824,292	1,837	6	2.50	1.89
Nepal	102	140,797	19,605	16	6.39	1.98
Nicaragua	7	130,000	3,999	8	8.13	2.15
Niger	21	1,267,000	7,984	10	2.40	1.28
Nigeria	427	923,768	112,163	24	7.00	2.16
Oman	8	212,457	1,559	2	0.00	0.00
Panama	13	75,517	2,466	5	9.20	0.75
Papua New Guinea	862	462,840	3,772	8	10.88	1.96
Paraguay	21	406,752	4,397	16	10.25	2.51
Peru	91	1,285,216	21,998	40	2.65	4.22
Phillipines	168	300,000	62,868	64	10.34	1.92
Saudi Arabia	8	2,149,690	14,691	10	0.40	0.92
Senegal	42	196,722	7,533	12	3.58	1.11
Sierra Leone	23	71,740	4,260	23	8.22	0.59
Solomon Is.	66	28,896	3,301	1	12.00	0.00
Somalia	14	637,657	7,691	28	3.00	1.69
South Africa	32	1,221,037	36,070	114	6.05	3.50
Sri Lanka	7	65,610	17,240	17	9.59	2.59
Sudan	134	2,505,813	25,941	43	4.02	2.82
Suriname	17	163,265	429	2	12.00	0.00
Tanzania	131	945,087	28,359	45	7.02	1.90
Thailand	82	513,115	56,293	54	8.04	1.57
Togo	43	56,785	3,643	11	7.91	1.78
UAE	9	83,600	1,629	6	0.83	0.69
Uganda	43	235,880	19,517	21	10.14	1.17
Vanuatu	111	12,189	163	4	12.00	0.00
Venezuela	40	912,050	20,226	44	7.98	2.73
Vietnam	88	331,689	68,183	40	8.80	1.59
Yemen	6	527,968	12,302	2	0.00	0.00
Zaire	219	2,344,858	36,672	16	9.44	1.90
Zambia	38	752,618	8,780	30	5.43	0.67

Country	Langs	Area	Pop.	Stations	MGS	Std
Zimbabwe	18	390,759	10,019	52	5.29	1.43

Notes: Langs: number of languages spoken by a resident population in the country, from Grimes (1993); Area: in km^2, from *UN Demographic Yearbook 1993*; Pop.: population in thousands, from *UN Demographic Yearbook 1993*; Stations: number of weather stations from which climate data have been taken; MGS: mean growing season, in months, from data in Wernstadt (1972); Std: Standard deviation of the growing season.

References

Abruzzi, W. S. (1982). Ecological theory and ethnic differentiation among human populations. *Current Anthropology*, 23: 13–21.

Abu-Lughod, J. L. (1989). *Before European Hegemony: The World System A.D. 1250–1350.* New York: Oxford University Press.

Adamu, M. (1976). The spread of Hausa culture in West Africa, 1700–1900. *Savanna*, 5: 3–14.

—— (1978). *The Hausa Factor in West African History.* Ibadan: Oxford University Press.

—— (1984). The Hausa and their neighbours in the central Sudan. In D. T. Niane (ed.), *UNESCO General History of Africa*, iv: *Africa from the Twelfth to the Sixteenth Centuries*, London: Heineman, 266–300.

Aitchison, J. (1991). *Language Change: Progress or Decay?* 2nd edn., Cambridge: Cambridge University Press.

Ammerman, A. and Cavalli-Sforza, L. L. (1973). A population model for the diffusion of early farming in Europe. In C. Renfrew (ed.), *The Explanation of Culture Change: Models in Prehistory*, London: Duckworth, 335–58.

Andersen, H. (1978). Perceptual and conceptual factors in abductive change. In J. Fisiak (ed.), *Recent Developments in Historical Phonology*, The Hague: Mouton, 1–23.

Axelrod, R. (1984). *The Evolution of Cooperation.* New York: Basic Books.

—— and Dion, D. (1988). The further evolution of cooperation. *Science*, 242: 1385–90.

Bailey, R. C., Head, G., Jenike, M., Owen, B., Rechtman, R., and Zechenter, E. (1989). Hunting and gathering in a tropical rainforest: is it possible? *American Anthropologist*, 91: 59–82.

Bailey, R., Jenike, M., Ellison, P., Bentley, B., Harrigan, A., and Peacock, N. (1992). The ecology of birth seasonality among agriculturalists in central Africa. *Journal of Biosocial Science*, 24: 393–412.

Bakker, P., and Mous, M. (1994) (eds.). *Mixed Languages: 15 Case Studies in Language Intertwining.* Amsterdam: Institute for Functional Research into Language and Language Use.

Barbujani, G., and Sokal, R. R. (1990). Zones of sharp genetic change in Europe are also linguistic boundaries. *Proceedings of the National Academy of Sciences of the U.S.A.*, 87: 1816–19.

Baron, N. S. (1977). *Language Acquisition and Historical Change.* Amsterdam: North Holland.

Barth, F. (1969). *Ethnic Groups and Boundaries.* London: Allen & Unwin.

Beecher, M. D., Campbell, S. E., and Stoddard, P.K. (1994). Correlation of song-learning and territory establishment strategies in the song sparrow. *Proceedings of the National Academy of Sciences of the U.S.A.*, 91: 1450–4.

Bellwood, P. (1997). Prehistoric cultural explanations for widespread language families. In P. McConvell and N. Evans (eds.), *Archaeology and Linguistics: Aboriginal Australia in Global Perspective*, Melbourne: Oxford University Press, 123–34.

Berg, E. (1976). *The Economic Impact of Drought and Inflation in the Sahel.* Ann Arbor, Mich.: Research for Economic Development.

Bergslund, K., and Vogt, H. (1962). On the validity of glottochronology. *Current Anthropology*, 3: 115–58.

Biraben, J.-N. (1979). Essai sur l'évolution du nombre des hommes. *Population*, 1: 13–24.

Birdsell, J. B. (1953). Some environmental and cultural factors influencing the structuring of Australian aboriginal populations. *American Naturalist*, 87: 171–207.

Bourhis, R. Y., and Giles, H. (1977). The language of intergroup distinctiveness. In H. Giles (ed.), *Language, Ethnicity and Intergroup Relations*, London: Academic Press, 119–34.

Boyd, R., and Richerson, P. J. (1985). *Culture and the Evolutionary Process.* Chicago: University of Chicago Press.

——— (1988). The evolution of reciprocity in sizeable groups. *Journal of Theoretical Biology*, 132: 337–56.

Braudel, F. de (1985). *Civilisation and Capitalism, 15th–18th Century*, i: *The Structures of Everyday Life.* London: Fontana.

Breton, R. J.-L. (1991). *Geolinguistics: Language Dynamics and Ethnolinguistic Geography.* Ottawa: University of Ottawa Press.

Brewis, A., Laycock, J., and Huntsman, J. (1996). Birth non-seasonality on the Pacific equator. *Current Anthropology*, 37: 843–50.

Brown, P. (1978). *Highland Peoples of New Guinea.* Cambridge: Cambridge University Press.

Bybee, J., Perkins, R., and Pagliucca, W. (1994). *The Evolution of Grammar. Tense, Aspect and Modality in the Languages of the World.* Chicago: University of Chicago Press.

Campbell, L. (1988). Review of Greenberg (1987). *Language*, 64: 591–615.

—— (1998). *Historical Linguistics: An Introduction.* Edinburgh: Edinburgh University Press.

—— Kaufman, T., and Smith-Stark, T. (1986). Mesoamerica as a linguistic area. *Language*, 92: 530–70.

Cann, R. L., Stoneking, M., and Wilson, A. C. (1987). Mitochondrial DNA and human evolution. *Nature*, 325: 31–5.

Caporael, L. R., Dawes, R. M., Orbell, J. M., and Van de Kragt, A. J. C. (1989). Selfishness examined: Cooperation in absence of egoistic incentives. *Behavioural and Brain Sciences*, 12: 683–739.

Carter, R., and McCarthy, M. (1995). Grammar and the spoken language. *Applied Linguistics*, 16: 141–58.

Casad, E. H. (1974). *Dialect Intelligibility Testing.* Norman, Okla.: Summer Institute of Linguistics.

Cashdan, E.(1985). Coping with risk: Reciprocity amongst the Basarwa of Northern Botswana. *Man*, NS 20: 454–74.

—— (1990) (ed.), *Risk and Uncertainty in Tribal and Peasant Economies.* Boulder, Colo.: Westview.

Cavalli-Sforza, L. L., and Feldman, M.W. (1981). *Cultural Transmission and Evolution: A Quantitative Approach.* Princeton: Princeton University Press.

Chambers, J. K. (1995). *Sociolinguistic Theory.* Oxford: Blackwell.

Chambers, R., Longhurst, R., and Pacey, A. (1981). *Seasonal Dimensions to Rural Poverty.* London: Frances Pinter.

Chomsky, N. A. (1965). *Aspects of the Theory of Syntax.* Cambridge, Mass.: MIT Press.

——(1986). *Knowledge of Language: Its Nature, Origin and Use.* New York: Praeger.

Clark, E. V. (1993). *The Lexicon in Acquisition.* Cambridge: Cambridge University Press.

Cohen, M. N. (1977). *The Food Crisis in Prehistory.* New Haven: Yale University Press.

——(1994). Demographic expansion: Causes and consequences. In T. Ingold (ed.), *Companion Encyclopaedia of Anthropology: Humanity, Culture and Social Life*, London: Routledge, 265–96.

Colson, E. (1979). In good years and bad: Food strategies of self-reliant societies. *Journal of Anthropological Research*, 35: 18–29.

Comrie, B. (1989). *Language Universals and Linguistic Typology.* 2nd edn., Oxford: Blackwell.

Condon, R. G., and Scaglion, R. (1982). The ecology of birth seasonality. *Human Ecology*, 10: 495–511.

Coulmas, F. (1992). *Language and Economy.* Oxford: Blackwell.

Croft, W. (1990). *Typology and Universals.* Cambridge: Cambridge University Press.

Crosby, A. W. (1986). *Ecological Imperialism: The Biological Expansion of Europe, 900–1900.* Cambridge: Cambridge University Press.

Curry, J. J. (1988). Seasonality, monetization, and occupational diversity in a Hausa village in Niger. In R. Huss-Ashmore, J. J. Curry and R. K. Hitchcock (eds.), *Coping with Seasonal Constraints*, Philadelphia: University Museum, University of Pennsylvania, 121–31.

Cutler, A., Hawkins, J. A., and Gilligan, G. (1985). The suffixing preference: A processing explanation. *Linguistics*, 23: 723–50.

Darwin, C. (1871). *The Descent of Man, and Selection in Relation to Sex.* London: Murray.

Date, E. M. and Lemon, R. E. (1993). Sound transmission—a basis for dialects in birdsong. *Behaviour*, 124: 291–312.

DeGarine, I., and Harrison, G. A. (1988) (eds.), *Coping with Uncertainty in the Food Supply.* Oxford: Oxford University Press.

Dennett, D. (1995). *Darwin's Dangerous Idea.* Harmondsworth: Penguin.

Diamond, J. (1997). *Guns, Germs and Steel: The Fate of Human Societies.* London: Jonathan Cape.

Dimmendaal, G. (1995). Do some languages have a multi-genetic or non-genetic origin? In R. Nicolai and F. Rottland (eds.), *Proceedings of the Fifth Nilo-Saharan Linguistics Colloqium*, Cologne: Koppe, 357–72.

Disner, S. F. (1984). Insights on vowel spacing. In I. Maddieson, *Patterns of Sounds*, Cambridge: Cambridge University Press, 136–55.

Dixon, R. M. W. (1997). *The Rise and Fall of Languages.* Cambridge: Cambridge University Press.

Dorian, N. (1993). A response to Ladefoged's other view of endangered languages. *Language*, 69: 575–9.

Dryer, M. S. (1989). Large linguistic areas and language sampling. *Studies in Language*, 13: 257–92.

——(1991). SVO languages and the OV:VO typology. *Journal of Linguistics*, 27: 443–82.

——(1992). The Greenbergian word-order correlations. *Language*, 68: 81–138.

Dunbar, R. I. M. (1993). Co-evolution of neocortex size, group size and language in humans. *Behavioural and Brain Sciences*, 16: 681–734.

——Duncan, N., and Nettle, D. (1995). Size and structure of freely-forming conversational groups. *Human Nature*, 6: 67–78.

Durkacz, V. E. (1983). *The Decline of the Celtic Languages*. Edinburgh: John Donald.

Dwyer, P. D., and Minnegal, M. (1992). Ecology and community dynamics of Kubo people in the tropical lowlands of Papua New Guinea. *Human Ecology*, 20: 21–55.

Dyen, I. (1990). Homomeric lexical classification. In P. Baldi (ed.), *Linguistic Change and Reconstruction Methodology*, Berlin: Mouton, 211–30.

Edgerton, R. B. (1992). *Sick Societies: Challenging the Myth of Primitive Harmony*. New York: Free Press.

Eldredge, N., and Gould, S. J. (1972). Punctuated equilibria: An alternative to phyletic gradualism. In T. J. M. Schopf (ed.), *Models in Paleobiology*, San Fransisco: Freeman & Cooper, 85–112.

Ellen, R. (1994). Modes of subsistence: From hunting and gathering to agriculture and pastoralism. In T. Ingold (ed.), *Companion Encyclopaedia of Anthropology: Humanity, Culture and Social Life*, London: Routledge, 197–225.

Embleton, S. M. (1986). *Statistics in Historical Linguistics*. Bochum: Brockmeyer.

——(1992). Historical linguistics: Mathematical concepts. In W. Bright (ed.), *International Encyclopaedia of Linguistics*, Oxford: Oxford University Press, ii. 131–4.

Enquist, M., and Leimar, O. (1993). The evolution of cooperation in mobile organisms. *Animal Behaviour*, 45: 747–57.

Feldman, R. E. (1968). Responses to compatriots and foreigners who seek assistance. *Journal of Personality and Social Psychology*, 10: 202–14.

Foley, R. A. and Fitzgerald, C. M. (1996). Is reproductive synchrony an evolutionarily stable strategy for hunter-gatherers? *Current Anthropology*, 37: 539–45.

Foley, W. A. (1986). *The Papuan Languages of New Guinea*. Cambridge: Cambridge University Press.

Fuchs, P. (1983). *Das Brot der Wüste: Socio-Ökonomie der Sahara, Kanuri von Fachi*. Wiesbaden: Steiner.

——(1984). Economic relations between the Sahara and the Sahel. *Current Anthropology*, 25: 116.

Gaertner, S. L., and Bickman, L. (1971). Effects of race on the elicitation of helping behaviour: the wrong number technique. *Journal of Personality and Social Psychology*, 20: 218–22.

Giles, H., Baker, S., and Fielding, G. (1975). Communication length as a behavioural index of accent prejudice. *International Journal of the Sociology of Language*, 6: 73–83.

Gimpel, J. (1976). *The Medieval Machine: The Industrial Revolution of the Middle Ages*. London: Victor Gollancz.

Grace, G. W. (1996). Regularity of change in what? In M. Durie and M. D. Ross (eds.), *The*

Comparative Method Reviewed: Regularity and Irregularity in Language Change, Oxford: Oxford University Press, 157–79.

Greenberg, J. H. (1963). *The Languages of Africa.* Bloomington, Ind.: Indiana University Press.

——(1966). Some universals of grammar with particular reference to the order of meaningful elements. In J. H. Greenberg (ed.), *Universals of Language*, 2nd edn., Cambridge, Mass.: MIT Press, 73–113.

——(1987). *Language in the Americas.* Stanford, Calif.: Stanford University Press.

Gregor, D. B. (1980). *Celtic: A Comparative Study of the Six Celtic Languages, their History, Literature and Destiny.* Cambridge: Oleander.

Grenoble, L. A., and Whaley, L. J. (1998) (eds.). *Endangered Languages: Current Issues and Future Prospects.* Cambridge: Cambridge University Press.

Grimes, B. F. (1993). *Ethnologue: The World's Languages.* 12th edn., Dallas: Summer Institute of Linguistics.

Guarisma, G. (1988). *Études Vouté (Langue Bantoïde du Cameroun).* Paris: SELAF.

Haiman, J. (1983). Iconic and economic motivation. *Language*, 59: 781–9.

Hale, K. (1992). On endangered languages and the safeguarding of diversity. *Language*, 68: 1–3.

Halstead, P., and O'Shea, J. (1989) (eds.). *Bad Year Economics: Cultural Responses to Risk and Uncertainty.* Cambridge: Cambridge University Press.

Harris, M. B., and Bardin, H. (1972). The language of altruism: The effects of language, dress and ethnic group. *Journal of Social Psychology*, 97: 37–41.

Hassan, F. (1981). *Demographic Archaeology.* New York: Academic Press.

Hawkins, J. A. (1983). *Word Order Universals.* New York: Academic Press.

——*A Performance Theory of Order and Constituency* (Cambridge: Cambridge University Press).

Hays, T. E. (1993). 'The New Guinea Highlands': Region, culture area, or fuzzy set? *Current Anthropology*, 34: 141–64.

Headland, T. N., and Reid, L. A. (1989). Hunter-gatherers and their neighbours from prehistory to the present. *Current Anthropology*, 30: 43–66.

Hermann-Pillath, C. (1994). Evolutionary rationality, 'Homo Economicus', and the foundations of the social order. *Journal of Social and Evolutionary Systems*, 17: 41–69.

Hill, P. (1982). *Dry Grain Farming Families: Hausaland (Nigeria) and Karnataka (India) Compared.* Cambridge: Cambridge University Press.

Hindley, R. (1990). *The Death of the Irish Language.* London: Routledge.

Hinton, G. E., and Nowlan, S. J. (1987). How learning can guide evolution. *Complex Systems*, 1: 495–502.

Hoffman, C. L. (1984). Punan foragers in the trading networks of Southeast Asia. In C. Schrire (ed.), *Past and Present in Hunter-Gatherer Studies*, Orlando: Academic Press, 123–49.

Hoijer, H. (1956). Lexicostatistics: A critique. *Language*, 32: 49–60.

Hombert, J. M. (1972). Towards a Theory of Tonogenesis: An Empirically, Physiologically and Perceptually Based Account of the Development of Tonal Contrasts in Languages. Ph.d. thesis, Univer Berkeley.

Hopper, P. J. (1990). Where do words come from? In W. Croft, K. Denning, and S.

Kemmer (eds.), *Studies in Typology and Diachrony for Joseph H. Greenberg*, Amsterdam: John Benjamins, 151–60.

Hudson, R. A. (1996). *Sociolinguistics*. 2nd edn., Cambridge: Cambridge University Press.

Hurford, J. R. (1987). *Language and Number: The Emergence of a Cognitive System*. Oxford: Blackwell.

——(1989). The biological evolution of the Saussurean sign as a component of the Language Acquisition Device. *Lingua*, 77: 187–222.

——(1991). The evolution of the critical period for language acquisition. *Cognition*, 40: 159–201.

Huss-Ashmore, R., Curry, J. J., and Hitchcock, R. K. (1988) (eds.), *Coping with Seasonal Constraints*. Philadelphia: University Museum, University of Pennsylvania.

Hymes, D. (1971). Foreword to M. Swadesh, *The Origin and Diversification of Language*, Chicago: Aldine Atherton, pp. v–x.

Jolly, P. (1996). Symbiotic interaction between black farmers and South-Eastern San: Implications for Southern African rock art studies, ethnographic analogy, and hunter-gatherer cultural identity. *Current Anthropology*, 37: 277–306.

Kaplan, H., Hill, K., and Hurtado, A. M. (1990). Risk, foraging, and food sharing amongst the Ache. In E. Cashdan (ed.), *Risk and Uncertainty in Tribal and Peasant Economies*, Boulder, Colo.: Westview, 107–43.

Kaye, J. D. (1989). *Phonology: A Cognitive View*. Hillsdale, NJ: Lawrence Erlbaum.

Keeley, L. H. (1996). *War before Civilization: The Myth of the Peaceful Savage*. Oxford: Oxford University Press.

Keller, R. (1994). *On Language Change: The Invisible Hand in Language*. London: Routledge.

Kimura, M. (1983). *The Neutral Theory of Molecular Evolution*. Cambridge: Cambridge University Press.

King, R. D. (1969). *Historical Linguistics and Generative Grammar*. Englewood Cliffs, NJ: Prentice Hall.

Kirby, S. (1993). Adaptive explanations for language universals: A model of Hawkins' performance theory. *Sprachtypologie und Universalienforschung*, 47: 186–210.

——(1995). Competing motivations and emergence: Explaining implicational hierarchies. *Edinburgh Occasional Papers in Linguistics*, 1.

——(1999). *Function, Selection and Innateness: The Emergence of Language Universals*. Oxford: Oxford University Press.

Kirch, P. V. (1991). Prehistoric exchange in Western Melanesia. *Annual Review of Anthropology*, 20: 141–65.

Krauss, M. (1992). The world's languages in crisis. *Language*, 68: 4–10.

Kulick, D. (1992). *Language Shift and Cultural Reproduction*. Cambridge: Cambridge University Press.

Kunitz, S. J. (1994). Disease and the destruction of indigenous populations. In T. Ingold (ed.), *Companion Encyclopaedia of Anthropology: Humanity, Culture and Social Life*, London: Routledge, 297–326.

Labov, W. (1963). The social motivation of a sound change. *Word*, 19: 273–309.

——(1972). *Sociolinguistic Patterns*. Philadelphia, Pa.: University of Pennsylvania Press.

——(1994). *Principles of Linguistic Change*, i: *Internal Factors*. Oxford: Blackwell.

Ladefoged, P. (1992). Another view of endangered languages. *Language*, 68: 809–11.

Lahr, M. M. (1994). The multiregional model of human evolution: A reassessment of its morphological basis. *Journal of Human Evolution*, 26: 23–56.

—— (1996). *The Evolution of Modern Human Diversity*. Cambridge: Cambridge University Press.

Lam, D., and Miron, J. (1991). Seasonality of births in human populations. *Social Biology*, 38: 51–78.

Lane, P. (1978). *The Industrial Revolution: The Birth of the Modern Age*. London: Weidenfeld & Nicolson.

Lang, K. (1992). Language and economists' theories of discrimination. *International Journal of the Sociology of Language*, 103: 165–83.

Last, M. (1985). The early kingdoms of the Nigerian savanna. In J. F. A. Ajayi and M. Crowder (eds.), *The History of West Africa*, 3rd edn., London: Longmans, i. 167–224.

Layton, R., Foley, R., and Williams, E. (1991). The transition between hunting and gathering and the specialized husbandry of resources: A socioecological approach. *Current Anthropology*, 32: 255–74.

Legge, K. (1989).Changing responses to drought amongst the Wodaabe of Niger. In P. Halstead and J. O'Shea (eds.), *Bad Year Economics: Cultural Responses to Risk and Uncertainty*, Cambridge: Cambridge University Press, 81–6.

Lehmann, W. P. (1962). *Historical Linguistics: An Introduction*. New York: Holt.

Le Houérou, H. N. (1989). *The Grazing Land Ecosystems of the African Sahel*. Ecological Studies 75. Berlin: Springer.

LePage, R. B. (1968). Problems of description in multilingual communities. *Transactions of the Philological Society*, 189–212.

Levin, M. (1994). The evolution of understanding—a genetic algorithm model of the evolution of communication. *Biosystems*, 36: 167–78.

Lieberman, P. (1963). Some effects of semantic and grammatical context on the production and perception of speech. *Language and Speech*, 6: 172–87.

Lightfoot, D. (1997). Catastrophic change and learning theory. *Lingua*, 100: 171–92.

Lindblom, B. (1986). Phonetic universals in vowel systems. In J. J. Ohala and J. J. Jaeger (eds.), *Experimental Phonology*, Dordrecht: Foris, 13–44.

—— (1990). Explaining phonetic variation: An outline of the H&H theory. In W. J. Hardcastle and A. Marchal (eds.), *Speech Production and Speech Modelling*, Dordrecht: Kluwer, 403–39.

—— and Maddieson, I. (1988). Phonetic universals in consonant systems. In L. M. Hyman and C. N. Li (eds.), *Language, Speech and Mind*, London: Routledge, 62–80.

—— Brownlee, S., Davies, B., and Moon, S. J. (1992). Speech transforms. *Speech Communication*, 11: 357–68.

—— Guion, S., Hura, S., Moon, S.-J., and Willerman, R. (1995). Is sound change adaptive? *Revista di Linguistica*, 7: 5–37.

Longacre, R. (1952). Five phonemic pitch levels in Trique. *Acta Linguistica*, 7: 62–82.

Lütdke, H. (1986). Esquisse d'une théorie du changement langagier. *La Linguistique*, 22: 3–46.

Mace, R., and Pagel, M. (1995). A latitudinal gradient in the density of human languages in North America. *Proceedings of the Royal Society of London, B*, 261: 117–21.

McMahon, A. M. S., and McMahon, R. (1995). Linguistics, genetics and archaeology: Internal and external evidence in the Amerind controversy. *Transactions of the Philological Society*, 93: 125–226.

Maddieson, I. (1984). *Patterns of Sounds*. Cambridge: Cambridge University Press.

Mann, M., and Dalby, D. (1987). *A Thesaurus of African Languages: A Classified and Annotated Bibliography of the Spoken Languages of Africa*. London: K. G. Saur.

Martinet, A. (1955). *Économie des changements phonétiques*. Berne: Francke.

Matisoff, J. M. (1973). Tonogenesis in South-East Asia. In L. M. Hyman (ed.), *Consonant Types and Tone*, Southern California Occasional Papers in Linguistics. Los Angeles: University of Southern California, 71–96.

—— (1990). On megalocomparison. *Language*, 66: 106–20.

Mayr, E. (1963). *Animal Species and Evolution*. Cambridge: Belknap Press.

Meggers, B. (1982). Archaeological evidence compatible with the model of forest fragmentation. In G. T. Prance (ed.), *Biological Diversification in the Tropics*, New York: Columbia University Press, 483–96.

Meggitt, M. J. (1973). System and sub-system: The *te* exchange cycle amongst the Mae Enga. *Human Ecology*, 1: 111–23.

Meillet, A. (1926). *Linguistique historique et linguistique générale*. Paris: Honor et Champion.

Milroy, L. (1980). *Language and Social Networks*. Oxford: Blackwell.

Minnis, P. E. (1985). *Social Adaptation to Food Stress: A Prehistoric South-Western Example*. Chicago: University of Chicago Press.

Morren, G. E. B. (1977). From hunting to herding: Pigs and the control of energy in montane New Guinea. In T. Bayliss-Smith and R. Feachem (eds.), *Subsistence and Survival in the Pacific*, London: Academic Press, 273–316.

Myers-Scotton, C. (1993). *Social Motivations for Code-Switching. Evidence from Africa*. Oxford: Oxford University Press.

Nettle, D. (1995). Segmental inventory size, word length, and communicative efficiency. *Linguistics*, 33: 359–67.

—— (1996a). The Evolution of Linguistic Diversity. Ph.D. thesis, University of London.

—— (1996b). Language diversity in West Africa: An ecological approach. *Journal of Anthropological Archaeology*, 15: 403–38.

—— (1998a). *The Fyem Language of Northern Nigeria*. Munich: Lincom Europa.

—— (1998b). Explaining global patterns of languages diversity. *Journal of Anthropological Archaeology* 17: 354–74.

—— (1998c). Coevolution of phonology and the lexicon in twelve languages of West Africa. *Journal of Quantitative Linguistics*, 5(3).

—— (forthcoming a). Using Social Impact Theory to simulate language change. *Lingua*, in press.

—— (forthcoming b). Is the rate of linguistic change constant? *Lingua*, in press.

—— (forthcoming c). Language variation and the evolution of societies. In C. Knight, C. Power, and R. I. M. Dunbar (eds.), *The Evolution of Culture*, Edinburgh: Edinburgh University Press.

—— and Dunbar, R. I. M. (1997). Social markers and the evolution of reciprocal exchange. *Current Anthropology*, 38: 93–8.

——and Romaine, S. (forthcoming). *Vanishing Voices: The Extinction of the World's Languages*. New York: Oxford University Press.

Nichols, J. (1986). Head-marking and dependent-marking grammar. *Language*, 62: 56–119.

——(1990). Linguistic diversity and the first settlement of the New World. *Language*, 66: 475–521.

——(1992). *Linguistic Diversity in Space and Time*. Chicago: University of Chicago Press.

——(1997). Sprung from two common sources: Sahul as a linguistic area. In P. McConvell and N. Evans (eds.), *Archaeology and Linguistics: Aboriginal Australia in Global Perspective*, Melbourne: Oxford University Press, 135–67.

Nicolas, G. (1967). Une forme atténuée du potlach en pays Hausa. *Économies et societés*, 2: 151–214.

Niddrie, D. L. (1971). The Carribean. In H. Blakemore and C. T. Smith (eds.), *Latin America: Geographical Perspectives*, London: Methuen, 73–120.

Oguntoyinbo, J. S. (1981). Climatic variability and food crop production in West Africa. *Geojournal*, 5: 139–50.

Otite, O. (1990). *Ethnic Pluralism and Ethnicity in Nigeria*. Ibadan: Shaneson.

Partridge, W. L. (1989). The human ecology of tropical land settlement in Latin America: Overview. In D. A. Schumann and W. L. Partridge (eds.), *The Human Ecology of Tropical Land Settlement in Latin America*, Boulder, Colo.: Westview, 3–19.

Patterson, O. (1975). Context and choice in ethnic allegiance: A theoretical framework and Carribean case study. In N. Glazer and D. P. Moynihan (eds.), *Ethnicity: Theory and Experience*, Cambridge, Mass.: Harvard University Press, 305–49.

Paul, H. (1880). *Prinzipien der Sprachegeschichte*. Halle: Niemeyer.

Perkins, R. D. (1992). *Deixis, Grammar and Culture*. Amsterdam: John Benjamins.

Peterson, G. E., and Barney, H. L. (1952). Control methods used in a study of the vowels. *Journal of the Acoustical Society of America*, 24: 175–84.

Pinker, S. (1994). *The Language Instinct*. Harmondsworth: Penguin.

——and Bloom, P. (1990). Natural language and natural selection. *Behavioural and Brain Sciences*, 13: 707–84.

Pollack, I. (1952). The information of elementary auditory displays. *Journal of the Acoustical Society of America*, 24: 745–9.

Pullum, G. K. (1981). Languages with Subject before Object: A comment and a catalogue. *Linguistics*, 19: 147–55.

——(1982). Letter. *Linguistics*, 20: 339–44.

——(1991). *The Great Eskimo Vocabulary Hoax, and Other Irreverent Essays on the Study of Language*. Chicago: University of Chicago Press.

Rappaport, R. (1968). *Pigs for the Ancestors*. New Haven: Yale University Press.

——(1971). The flow of energy in an agricultural society. *Scientific American*, 225: 116–32.

Raynault, C. (1977). Aspects socio-économiques de la préparation et de la circulation de la nourriture dans un village Hausa (Niger). *Cahiers d'Études africaines*, 68/17: 569–97.

Relethford, J. H. (1995). Genetics and modern human origins. *Evolutionary Anthropology*, 4: 53–63.

Rempel, H. (1981). Seasonal out-migration and rural poverty. In R. Chambers, R.

Longhurst, and A. Pacey (eds.), *Seasonal Dimensions to Rural Poverty*, London: Frances Pinter, 210–13.

Renfrew, C. (1987). *Archaeology and Language: The Puzzle of Indo-European Origins.* London: Jonathan Cape.

——(1991). Before Babel: Speculations on the origin of linguistic diversity. *Cambridge Archeological Journal*, 1: 3–23.

Ridley, M. (1996). *The Origins of Virtue.* Harmondsworth: Penguin.

Ringe, D. (1992). On calculating the factor of chance in language comparison. *Transactions of the American Philosophical Society*, 82: 1–110.

Roberts, J. M., Moore, C. C., and Romney, A. K. (1995). Predicting material culture among New Guinea villages from propinquity and language: A log-linear approach. *Current Anthropology*, 36: 769–88.

Roberts, R. G., Jones, R., and Smith, M. A. (1990). Thermoluminescence dating of a 50,000 year old human occupation site in northern Australia. *Nature*, 345: 153–6.

Robins, R. H., and Uhlenbeck, E. M. (1991) (eds.). *Endangered Languages.* Oxford: Berg.

Rogers, A. R., and Jorde, L. B. (1995). Genetic evidence on modern human origins. *Human Biology*, 67: 1–36.

Romaine, S. (1994). *Language in Society: An Introduction to Sociolinguistics.* Oxford: Oxford University Press.

Rosner, B. S., and Pickering, J. B. (1991). *Vowel Perception and Production.* Oxford: Oxford University Press.

Ross, M. D. (1994). Areal phonological features in north central New Ireland. In T. Dutton and D. Tryon (eds.), *Language Contact and Change in the Austroneisan World*, Berlin: Mouton de Gruyter, 551–72.

——(1996). Contact induced change and the comparative method: Cases from Papua New Guinea. In M. Durie and M. D. Ross (eds.), *The Comparative Method Reviewed: Regularity and Irregularity in Language Change*, Oxford: Oxford University Press, 180–217.

Ruhlen, M. (1987). *A Guide to the World's Languages*, i: *Classification.* London: Edward Arnold.

Sampson, G. (1980). *Schools of Linguistics: Competition and Evolution.* London: Hutchinson.

Sands, B. E. (1995). Evaluating Claims of Distant Linguistic Relationship: The Case of Khoisan. Ph.D. thesis, UCLA.

Sapir, E. (1921/1970). *Language.* London: Harcourt, Brace & World.

Saussure, F. de (1916). *Cours de linguistique générale.* Paris: Payot.

Scott, E. P. (1976). *Indigenous Systems of Exchange and Decision-Making among Smallholders in Rural Hausaland.* Ann Arbor: Department of Geography Publications, University of Michigan.

Shaw, B. D. (1996). Seasons of death: Aspects of mortality in ancient Rome. *Journal of Roman Studies*, 86: 100–38.

Shott, M. J. (1992). On recent trends in the anthropology of foragers: Kalahari revisionism and its archaeological implications. *Man*, 27: 843–71.

Sigmund, K. (1995). *Games of Life: Explorations in Ecology, Evolution, and Behaviour.* Oxford: Oxford University Press.

Simmons, E. B. (1981). A case study in food production, sale, and distribution. In R. Chambers, R. Longhurst, and A. Pacey (eds.), *Seasonal Dimensions to Rural Poverty*, London: Frances Pinter, 210–13.

Sokal, R. R., and Crovello, T. J. (1970). The biological species concept: A critical evaluation. *American Naturalist*, 104: 127–53.

Solway, J. S., and Lee, R. B. (1990). Foragers, genuine or spurious? Situating the Kalahari San in history. *Current Anthropology*, 31: 109–46.

Sorenson, A. P. (1971). Multi-lingualism in the Northwest Amazon. *American Anthropologist*, 69: 670–84.

Stevens, G. C. (1989). The latitudinal gradient in species range: How so many species co-exist in the tropics. *American Naturalist*, 133: 240–56.

Stoneking, M. (1993). DNA and recent human evolution. *Evolutionary Anthropology*, 2: 60–73.

Swadesh, M. (1950). Salish internal relationships. *International Journal of American Linguistics*, 16: 157–67.

Swift, J. (1973). Disaster and a Sahelain nomad economy. In D. Dalby and R. J. Harrison-Church (eds.), *Drought in Africa*, London: Centre for African Studies, SOAS, 71–8.

——(1986). The economics of production and exchange in West African pastoral societies. In M. J. Adamu and A. H. M. Kirk-Greene (eds.), *Pastoralists of the West African Savanna*. Manchester: Manchester University Press.

Teeter, K. V. (1963). Lexicostatistics and genetic relationship. *Language*, 39: 638–48.

Thomason, S. G., and Kaufman, T. (1988). *Language Contact, Creolization, and Genetic Linguistics*. Berkeley and Los Angeles: University of California Press.

Tomlin, R. (1986). *Basic Constituent Orders: Functional Principles*. London: Croom Helm.

Trask, R. L. (1996). *Historical Linguistics*. London: Edward Arnold.

Tubaro, P. L., Segura, E. T., and Handford, P. (1993). Geographic variation in the song of the rufous-coloured songbird in Eastern Argentina. *Condor*, 95: 588–95.

Waddell, E. (1975). How the Enga cope with frost: Responses to climatic perturbations in the Central Highlands of New Guinea. *Human Ecology*, 3: 249–75.

Walsh, R. P. D. (1981). The nature of climatic seasonality. In R. Chambers, R. Longhurst, and A. Pacey (eds.), *Seasonal Dimensions to Rural Poverty*, London: Frances Pinter, 11–20.

Watts, M. (1983). *Silent Violence: Food, Famine and the Peasantry in Northern Nigeria*. Berkeley and Los Angeles: University of California Press.

Weinreich, U., Labov, W., and Herzog, M. I. (1968). Empirical foundations for a theory of language change. In W. P. Lehmann (ed.), *Directions for Historical Linguistics*, Austin, Tex.: University of Texas Press, 95–188.

Wernstadt, F. L. (1972). *World Climatic Data*. Lemont, Pa.: Climatic Data Press.

Wheeler, M., and Debourcier, P. (1995). How not to murder your neighbor—using synthetic behavioral ecology to study aggressive signaling. *Adaptive Behavior*, 3: 273–309.

White, J. P., and Mulvaney, D. J. (1987). How many people? In D. J. Mulvaney and J. P. White (eds.), *Australians to 1788*. Broadway, NSW: Fairfax, Syme & Weldon Associates.

Wiessner, P. (1977). Hxaro. A regional system of reciprocity for reducing risk among the !Kung San. Ph.D. Thesis, University of Michigan.

Winterhalder, B. (1986). Diet choice, risk, and food-sharing in a stochastic environment. *Journal of Anthropological Archaeology*, 5: 369–92.

——(1990). Open field, common pot: Harvest variability and risk avoidance in agricultural and foraging societies. In E. Cashdan (ed.), *Risk and Uncertainty in Tribal and Peasant Economies*, Boulder, Colo.: Westview, 67–88.

Wolf, E. (1982). *Europe and the People without History.* Berkeley and Los Angeles: University of California Press.

——(1992). Perilous ideas: Race, culture, people. *Current Anthropology*, 34: 141–64.

Wolff, H. (1959). Intelligibility and inter-ethnic attitudes. *Anthropological Linguistics*, 1: 34–41.

Wolpoff, M. H. (1989). Multiregional evolution: The fossil alternative to Eden. In P. Mellars and C. B. Stringer (eds.), *The Human Revolution: Behavioural and Biological Perspectives on the Evolution of Modern Humans*, Edinburgh: Edinburgh University Press, 62–108.

——(1996). Interpretations of multiregional evolution. *Science*, 274: 704–6.

Woodburn, J. (1986). African hunter-gatherer social organization: Is it best understood as a product of encapsulation? In T. Ingold, D. Riches, and J. Woodburn (eds.), *Hunters and Gatherers*, Oxford: Berg, i. 31–64.

World Bank (1995). *World Development Report, 1995.* Oxford: Oxford University Press for the World Bank.

Yengoyan, A. A. (1968). Demographic and ecological influences on Aboriginal Australian marriage sections. In R. B. Lee and I. Devore (eds.), *Man the Hunter*, New York: Aldine, 185–99.

Zvelebil, M., and Zvelebil, K. V. (1988). Agricultural transitions and Indo-European dispersals. *Antiquity*, 62: 574–83.

Index